LIVING IN BLISS

ACHIEVE A BALANCED EXISTENCE OF BODY, MIND, AND SPIRIT

LIVING IN BLISS

ACHIEVE A BALANCED EXISTENCE OF BODY, MIND, AND SPIRIT

PETE SACCO

LIVING IN BLISS © 2025 by Pete Sacco. All rights reserved.

Printed in the United States of America

Published by Igniting Souls
PO Box 43, Powell, OH 43065
IgnitingSouls.com

This book contains material protected under international and federal copyright laws and treaties. Any unauthorized reprint or use of this material is prohibited. No part of this book may be reproduced or transmitted in any form or by any means, electronic or mechanical, including photocopying, recording, or by any information storage and retrieval system, without express written permission from the author.

LCCN: 2024918816
Paperback ISBN: 978-1-63680-371-5
Hardcover ISBN: 978-1-63680-372-2
e-book ISBN: 978-1-63680-373-9

Available in paperback, hardcover, e-book, and audiobook.

Any Internet addresses (websites, blogs, etc.) and telephone numbers printed in this book are offered as a resource. They are not intended in any way to be or imply an endorsement by Igniting Souls, nor does Igniting Souls vouch for the content of these sites and numbers for the life of this book.

Some names and identifying details may have been changed to protect the privacy of individuals.

The superscript symbol IP listed throughout this book is known as the unique certification mark created and owned by Instant IP™. Its use signifies that the corresponding expression (words, phrases, chart, graph, etc.) has been protected by Instant IP™ via smart contract. Instant IP™ is designed with the patented smart contract solution (US Patent: 11,928,748), which creates an immutable time-stamped first layer and fast layer identifying the moment in time an idea is filed on the blockchain. This solution can be used in defending intellectual property protection. Infringing upon the respective intellectual property, i.e., IP, is subject to and punishable in a court of law.

To my three beautiful daughters
Emilia, **Giavana**, and **Siena**

You are the light that guides my path, the inspiration behind my pursuit of a life well-lived. Because of you, I strive each day to be a better man, a more present father, and a more compassionate soul. Your laughter reminds me of the joy in simplicity, your curiosity fuels my own thirst for wisdom, and your love is the greatest gift I could ever receive. This book exists because of you, just as my purpose is made richer by your presence in the world. May you always walk in truth, love, joy, and limitless possibility.

With all my heart, this is for you.

Access Your Free Bonuses

Enjoy Exclusive Content,
Supplemental Material, Videos, and More

PeteSacco.com

Table of Contents

Note to the Reader............................ ix

Part 1: The Need for Change

Chapter 1: The Journey Begins..................... 3
Chapter 2: The Roadmap for Change............... 13

Part 2: Balancing Body, Mind, and Spirit

Chapter 3: Healing the Body 29
Chapter 4: Healing the Mind 42
Chapter 5: Discover Your Superpowers............. 53
Chapter 6: Live Your Core Values 58
Chapter 7: Tools for Change..................... 67
Chapter 8: Healing the Spirit 79
Chapter 9: Achieving Body, Mind, and Spirit Harmony.. 86

Part 3: Achieving Enlightenment

Chapter 10: The Path to Enlightenment 95
Chapter 11: Sharing the Light 103

Endnotes 107
Acknowledgments 115
About the Author............................. 119

Note to the Reader

This is what I believe:

1. **We are not our bodies, not our feelings or emotions, and not our minds. We are pure conscious energy.**[IP] We have existed for all time, are here now in this earthly form, and will continue to exist for all time. In the now, our consciousness communicates with the information contained in the vast background energy that connects everything—universal knowledge. It is the vacuum energy described in quantum mechanics and perhaps related to the dark energy responsible for the expansion of the Universe.

2. **Our genes are not our destiny.** If we control our environment, we can control our health and happiness. Epigenetics and neuroplasticity will take care of the rest by changing our bodies and minds.

3. **We are not limited by time and space.** Pure consciousness is fundamental to the Universe. Matter, energy, time, and space are emergent or manifestations of consciousness rather than the other way

around. In keeping with quantum mechanics, we manifest events in the now and the future by being active observers of the Universe of infinite possibilities, thereby collapsing our intentions into reality. Further, we can amplify these intentions with the collective consciousness of a group.

I am not alone in my beliefs. It can easily be argued that because of the proliferation of knowledge and the ease of obtaining it, more people are achieving, seeking, and teaching the path to Enlightenment than ever before.

In the end, everyone has their own path to Enlightenment. Imagine a life where your body vibrates with vitality, your mind is clear and focused, and your spirit radiates peace and purpose. Achieving this balance is possible and deeply fulfilling—it is the essence of living in bliss. Let this book be your guide. By aligning your thoughts, actions, and inner essence, you can unlock profound joy, clarity, and resilience. This journey is your birthright: to thrive in harmony with your higher self and the world around you and awaken to the extraordinary potential of a life lived in balance.

PART 1

The Need for Change

Wisdom is knowing I am nothing. Love is knowing I am everything. And between the two, my life moves.

—Sri Nisargadatta Maharaj

1

The Journey Begins

From Technologist to Mystic

What is bliss? An outside observer might describe my life as blissful. My wife and I are blessed with three young daughters. I have a wonderful relationship with my grown son, and his family has made me a grandfather. I am healthy and successful in my profession and will probably live and work well into my hundreds. In short, I have found my purpose and am living it out.

But if you had known me twenty years ago, you would never have used the word "bliss" to describe my life. I was utterly disconnected from my mind, body, and spiritual self, bound up in a loveless marriage, and estranged from my son. On top of it all, I weighed well over three hundred fifty pounds and suffered from severe health issues.

So how did I get here? It took a fundamental change. To start any journey toward enlightenment or self-betterment, you have to reach a transformative low. It's cliche to say, "I'm at the end of my rope," but there's no better illustration. We all reach the point where we either fall or start climbing back up. And everyone's low is different. Mine was just painful enough to force me into action.

When I was thirty-eight, I was diagnosed with borderline diabetes. I'll never forget the moment after I turned forty when my doctor walked into the room clapping. A little startled, I asked, "What's up?"

"Congratulations, Pete," she said. "You've joined the ranks of the unhealthy. Here's your blood pressure medication, your cholesterol medication, and your blood sugar medications. You're officially type-2 diabetic. Keep it up." Shocked by her frankness, I didn't say a word.

"Yes, your paternal grandparents lived into their nineties, but your maternal grandparents were dead in their sixties and early seventies. If you keep going this way, you'll be dead too soon too."

As blunt and shocking as this interaction was, it did not result in the great transformation it could have. It was revelatory, but I didn't truly hit rock bottom until three years later. I share this interaction to illustrate what the beginning of transformation looks like. It starts with pain and truth. This doctor expressed the truth better than I could have. She saw me for who I was and where I was, and she tried to set me on the path toward health by making me aware of my condition. This is what I hope to do for you. Maybe you have already hit your rock bottom, and you're looking for a hand to help you climb the rope. If you haven't yet decided that change is necessary, I hope to make your rock bottom a little shallower than mine was.

I like to believe that we don't all have to experience something traumatic or devastating to inspire transformation. My pain was undoubtedly minor compared to many. Regardless of how much pain you must face before you turn toward enlightenment, we all must surrender to the pain and find enlightenment in that moment. So, as I share a mountaintop vision of the bliss possible for everyone, my hope is to inspire you to surrender to whatever pain you now face and start your journey toward enlightenment now. Like Robert Pirsig wrote in his critically acclaimed novel, *Zen and the Art of Motorcycle Maintenance*, "The only Zen you can find on the tops of mountains is the Zen you bring up there."[1]

The Awakening: Recognizing the Call to a Higher Purpose

When I finally hit the wall in my forties, I hit it hard. I knew without a doubt: "I can't do this any longer." It was time to turn my life around, but I needed a goal to reach for. I had to stop the pain—physical, emotional, and mental—it was unsustainable. But I couldn't simply stop everything going wrong in my life; I had to replace it with something. I needed to seek some semblance of a "good life."

On a practical level, these conclusions meant I had to get healthy. I needed to divorce my now ex-wife for both our sakes. I needed to build a relationship with my son. I knew I wanted to remarry, to share my life with someone. I had no idea who that would be when I made the decision, but I knew I would remarry. We would have children, and I would raise those children with my new ideals. If I failed at parenting this time around, at least it would be by my own hand. Lastly, I was determined to learn what it takes to be happy and make it an everlasting part of the rest of my life as well as those lives around me.

We need lofty goals to get anywhere, but I didn't achieve these goals by dramatic gestures. You can't lose a hundred pounds by not eating for the rest of your life. You take it little by little, breaking it up into bite-sized chunks. No one described this better than James Clear in *Atomic Habits*. If you improve by one percent every day, your growth throughout the year is astronomical.[2] Change occurs when you build good habits and break bad ones. Bill Gates is attributed with saying, "Most people overestimate what they can do in one year and underestimate what they can do in ten years."[3] I'll take that a step further and add that we overestimate what we can accomplish in a day and underestimate what we can accomplish in a year.

Once I clarified my plan and decisions, I followed through—*Atomic Habits* style, even though Clear wouldn't write his book for almost another decade! I was on track to accomplish everything I set out to do, just as described above. I was divorced, fit, and starting to put myself out there again. Could I actually attract love? Can I build a relationship with my son Peter? Everything was hopeful. Then I found out this was not the end of the story: everything crashed to the ground yet again.

By 2015, I had met my wife, and we were about to start a family. I had decided not to coach any longer to free myself up to invest in the children. My whole life, coaching, mentoring, and motivating others was my joy. I found my identity in it, and it gave me life. I knew it was right to give it up, but it was a huge loss. I couldn't use the coaching mentality on my wife—that's not what wives are for! We were one; our job was to shepherd our children through life together. I might be able to repurpose my love for mentoring as I raised my girls, but they were not born yet, much less in need of motivational guidance. So, this void started to open up regarding my purpose and direction.

To make matters worse, my company started to struggle financially. In retrospect, this all hit me way harder than it should have. My life, even then, was still better than ninety-nine percent of people on the planet. At the time, though, my world faced an utter breakdown, and it led to bouts of severe anxiety.

Now, I'm a smart guy. I knew I needed help. So I did some research and stumbled across Cognitive Behavioral Therapy (CBT). Cognitive refers to the way we think, Behavioral refers to the actions we take, and, of course, Therapy combines the two and helps us make sense of things. CBT treatment focuses on identifying and modifying negative patterns of thought, beliefs, and behaviors that contribute to emotional distress. The premise of CBT is that our thoughts, feelings, and behaviors are interconnected and that changing maladaptive thinking patterns can lead to changes in feelings and behaviors. David Glaser, a local Licensed Clinical Social Worker (LCSM) specializing in CBT, was instrumental in my rebound.

Any therapy is difficult at first. It's a human tendency to bury your soul so deep no one can find it, and I was very experienced with therapists—marriage therapists, at least. After a few months of sessions, David gave me his diagnosis. "You have megalomaniac tendencies with an inferiority complex," meaning I have an inflated sense of self-importance (ego) and an obsessive desire for attention and control, as well as deep-seated insecurities. This inner conflict manifested as fear of inadequacy, rejection, and failure. My coping mechanism is typically an exaggerated display of superiority and dominance, which acts as a mask to hide my feelings of vulnerability and self-doubt. But David kept digging. He asked simple questions in an infuriating way that cut right through my hesitancy. Our meetings went something like this:

"What's the problem, Pete?"

"Well, the company is not doing well."

"Okay, what would it mean if it keeps going south?"

"If it goes bad, then I've disappointed all the people I work for because they are expecting me to lead them and survive as a company."

"And what might happen then?"

"I guess they would all lose their jobs. They'd have to all go out and find something new. I would too—I'd have to pick up the pieces and figure something out."

"Okay, well, what would you do then?"

"Oh, I'd probably be fine. It would be tough, but I've got other things I could pursue. I just know it would be a huge letdown for my wife."

> **Pete, don't make the events of your life, which you cannot control, your problems.**

David responded incredulously, "Really? Have you ever asked her? If you lost your job tomorrow, would she really care about the money you're not making? Does she care whether you're living in a big house or a little shack?"

"No, not at all."

"Alright, then, what's the problem?" And this is when he handed me the Holy Grail. He said, "Pete, don't make the events of your life, which you cannot control, your problems."

There it was: my first spiritual realization. These things plaguing me were simply the events of my life. Life isn't about my mental state; it's not about my emotional state; it's not about my body. There's something more. I didn't know what it was then, but that realization bounced me back.

The Rubber Ball

I use the words "bounce back" very intentionally. Around the time I discovered this new spiritual reality, I realized my life had followed a specific pattern. Imagine holding a rubber ball and throwing it up as high as you can. This initial toss is everything we aspire to do. For me, my first marriage and early professional aspirations were my first mighty heave into the sky. For some of us, that ball goes really high as we achieve great things. But inevitably, gravity will cause it to crash to the ground.

The episode with my therapist was the first time I hit bottom. As I've shared, the first bounce was the most powerful. During that phase, my life was utterly transformed. But again, what happens each time a rubber ball bounces up? It falls again. My second bounce happened when I quit coaching and my business suffered.

Here's the key to it all, though. Even if you feel right now that you could handle bouncing back forever, you don't have to. When a rubber ball bounces, the intervals between the bounces get shorter. It doesn't bounce as high each time. Each time the ball goes up, we know it will come back down, but hitting the ground will hurt less and less. And yet we are always moving forward.

Self-improvement is like the rubber ball. Every moment of growth is that ball flinging into the air, but there will always be another drop. The important thing is to recognize that it's not about the highs and the lows. Both are fleeting. Neither will last forever, or usually, for very long. Despite my analogy of throwing a ball in the air, I've learned it's not like that at all. We have little control over the highs and lows of our lives. The best we can do is experience the moments for what they are—temporary moments in time. More important is to recognize that the ball has always moved forward. No matter what, there is always progress. Life is forever changing.

What I eventually came to realize at this point in my life is that it was less like throwing a bouncing ball along the pavement and more like a cork bobbing on waves in the ocean—just intermittent swells of peaks and valleys, perpetually moving forward, over which we have no control. When you know that life is not about its highs and lows but more about living in the present moment, you will start to realize you can embrace your existence regardless of your ups and downs.[IP]

There is an infinite sky above you and a near-infinite sea below you; you are the ripples on the waves of life. What's more, there is no true distinction between the ocean and waves and sky. Everything is one.

We will continue to return to this picture. It was the key perspective that empowered me to pursue my purpose with success. When you are no longer concerned with the events external to you, enlightenment is within reach.

> **Happiness is the surrender of both good and bad.[IP] I am happy when I understand I don't need the good or the bad. Neither affects me anymore.**

What does this have to do with the call to a higher purpose? Many people believe that life's purpose has to do with happiness. When the ball first dropped for me, pursuing happiness was part of what bounced me back. Later, though, I reconsidered the meaning of happiness.

I was on vacation with some friends, and we were discussing the core value of purpose. When asked, one friend explained his purpose was to live a life of happiness. Although a life of happiness sounds pretty good, I had to debate him

The Journey Begins

on it. Happiness—as most people comprehend it—can't be a purpose. It's fleeting. It's based on circumstance. You can't live a life of just happiness because you will constantly be disappointed by the events of life. Put another way, the ball is going to bounce.

So, do we have to give up on ever being happy? Thankfully, no. There is another way to understand happiness. Happiness is the surrender of both good and bad.[IP] I am happy when I understand I don't need the good or the bad. Neither affects me anymore.

I play tennis like a madman. I love the game, but I started to get frustrated at one point because my skills had plateaued. It felt impossible to get any better. Then, as I talked with a friend about life, he said something profound: "Living in this sense of reality is not just about forgetting the bad. You also have to forget the good because the good can't be perpetuated."

Everything clicked for me. If I hit a bad shot two seconds ago, I needed to ignore it so it didn't influence my next one. If I hit a good shot, I can't allow that to influence my next shot, either. If I did, I might expect my next shot to be better than the last when, in reality, it could easily be much worse. I now

Wisdom is recognizing the awesomeness, not only in the moments of greatness, but in the moments of the mundane.[IP]

treat every point of my tennis game as if I had never played it before and enjoy every second. My abilities don't plateau because all that matters is this moment right now.

It's not about how happy or sad I can be. That perspective led only to anxiety and my second low. As Buddha taught, nothing is permanent. We all live in an ever-changing world. If we surrender the highs and surrender the lows, all we have left is progressing through life, realizing that progression in itself is wondrous.

David and CBT helped me immeasurably. However, what I didn't know at this time was that the internal fears and self-doubt that led to my anxiety were actually much more deeply imprinted in me as a result of my genetic makeup, my upbringing, and the childhood experiences that formed my prefrontal cortex. But more about that in Part Two.

At this point, however, I realized wisdom is recognizing the awesomeness, not only in the moments of greatness, but in the moments of the mundane.[IP] That is the secret.

2

The Roadmap for Change

Everything Is Connected

When we talk about the bouncing ball metaphor, the end result is the realization that everything—sea, waves, sky, space, stars, galaxies, the Universe—is all the same. Everything is made of matter, energy, and information—the quantum field of potentiality and infinite possibilities, a field of pure potential that can be influenced by consciousness. I believe the quantum field and pure consciousness are interconnected and are *fundamental* to the Universe. Consciousness plays a role in shaping the quantum field, making reality as we perceive it.

Nicola Tesla has been credited with saying, "If you want to find the secrets of the Universe, think in terms of energy, frequency, and vibration."[4] He added, "Throughout space, there is energy. Is this energy static or kinetic? If static, our hopes are in vain; if kinetic—and this we know it is, for certain—then it is a mere question of time when men will succeed in attaching their machinery to the very wheelwork of nature."[5] So, we can surmise that everything must be connected, but universal connectivity leads to more questions.

> I believe the quantum field and pure consciousness are interconnected and are *fundamental* to the Universe. Consciousness plays a role in shaping the quantum field, making reality as we perceive it.

You and I are both included in that "everythingness." Consciousness is the seat of our eternal self[IP] and has been called many things throughout history—God, divinity, the soul, the formless self, energy being, spiritual self, conscious receiver, higher self, overself, the observer, Atman, and endless others. To me, they all describe the same eternal "You."

The concept that all things are interconnected and pure consciousness connects the eternal self to this interconnectedness is a profound and recurring theme in many religious, spiritual, and philosophical traditions across civilizations, from Judaic Mysticism to Ancient Greek and Roman religions to Australian Aboriginal beliefs. For a short survey of these religions, scan the QR code below.

This interconnectedness through pure consciousness forms a central tenet across numerous civilizations, reflecting humanity's persistent pursuit of understanding our intrinsic connection to everything that exists.

The Model of Man: Body-Self, Mind-Body Self, and Mental Self

If we don't know what we are dealing with, we can never control it. We must start with a model of man. Many people have created models of human existence over the years, with varying degrees of success and accuracy. Michael Singer's framework is quite good, but I've amended it into a new, Comprehensive Model of Man^{IP}.

We primarily think of our "self" as our body. We call this the body-self or the animal self. This self inhabits the physical plane and primarily interacts with our senses of touch, sight, sound, smell, and taste. We gather data through the senses and conceptualize ourselves as having dimension and interaction as a physical body.

The next level of self is emotional, or what I like to refer to as the mind-body self. Emotions are closely tied to both the animal self and the mental self, which we will discuss further along because we manifest feelings in our physical body. These feelings are interpreted by the mind and stored in our memory as experiences. Feelings are energy in motion channeled through our body's chakras, or energy centers.

In general, emotion flows from the Root chakra up through the rest of the body, but the flow can become blocked due to many factors. We experience feelings through our bodies, but we also perceive emotion through our consciousness, and the intersection of those experiences forms the true emotional or mind-body self.

The emotional plane is the range of energy vibrations above what is normally detectable by the five senses but below the vibration rate of the mental plane. The Hawkins Energy Scale, created by Dr. David R. Hawkins and presented in his book *Power vs. Force*, ranks human emotions and states of consciousness on a scale from 0 to 1000.[6] According to Hawkins, higher frequencies on this scale correspond to greater levels of consciousness and positivity, while lower frequencies align with negative emotions or states. However, despite the intriguing philosophical and experiential insights it offers, the Hawkins Energy Scale is not widely recognized or verified within the scientific community. Regardless, the Hawkins Energy Scale can be a useful tool for personal growth and reflection on emotional states.

If we take a step higher into the mental plane, we find our mental self. As you might imagine, the mental self is complex. A common understanding of the mental versus physical self is "My body is how I perceive myself, but my mind is actually me." While there is a kernel of truth to it, this is a dramatic oversimplification.

Dandapani, an ex-Hindu priest, aptly describes the mind as a dark mansion in his book *The Power of Unwavering Focus*.[7] If you found yourself in this mansion, you would see nothing but long hallways with hundreds and thousands of closed doors. If you could open a door, you would find that each room stores certain memories, experiences, or intellectual capacities. Even if you forced a door open, though, you wouldn't be able to see inside. But every once in a while, a great flood light illuminates what's inside the rooms behind the doors.

This light is your conscious awareness and dictates which rooms are used and how frequently. When something happens, it might elicit an emotional reaction, but that emotion actually just sits there in a darkened room until the light of your awareness focuses on it. Focused concentration is a skill we can all cultivate through the practice of meditation. Once mastered, you have utter control over which rooms are illuminated in your mind at any given moment.

You have a consciously aware mind—the floodlight in the mansion—but you also have subconscious and unconscious minds. They are akin to normal house functions such as heating, cooling, and running water. They happen, and we know they happen, but we don't have to actively operate them to make sure they work.

The other common understanding of how the mind works is from Sigmund Freud's theory of personality, which involves three components: id, ego, and superego. Most have heard these terms, but the actual meanings tend to get obscured. The id represents the instinctual desire for pleasure and immediate gratification. As an example, the id craves the cake and urges you to eat it right away to satisfy hunger and the pleasure of taste, without thinking of the consequences like weight gain.

The superego represents our moral values and societal norms. It counters the id by reminding us that eating the cake might violate our commitment to staying healthy or adhering to our diet. It invokes feelings of guilt or shame, urging us to resist temptation and uphold discipline.

According to Freud, the ego, which mediates between the id and the superego, tries to find a compromise. It acknowledges the id's desire for the cake but also considers the superego's demand for self-control. The ego might suggest a middle ground—perhaps allowing a smaller portion of cake or delaying the indulgence until after you've completed a workout.

However, in my experience, this doesn't seem exactly right. American social psychologist and author Jonathan David Haidt uses a different analogy to describe the ego in his book *The Happiness Hypothesis*.[8] He compares the mind to a rider on an elephant, where the elephant represents the automatic, emotional, and unconscious processes (similar to Freud's id), and the rider is the conscious, rational mind (closer to Freud's ego).

In this metaphor, the rider (ego) tries to steer the elephant using reason and willpower. However, the rider's control is limited because the elephant (representing our powerful emotions, instincts, and habitual responses) often drives behavior. While the rider can guide and direct the elephant at times, it can be difficult for the rider to control it when the elephant has strong desires or instincts.

Haidt suggests that much of our behavior is driven by this emotional elephant, with the rider rationalizing decisions after the fact rather than truly being in control. The interplay here illustrates the ego's role as a reasoning force, but one that is often less powerful than we believe when faced with the deep emotional forces of our subconscious.

This view contrasts Freud's idea of the ego being a mediator between the id and superego. Haidt emphasizes the limited control of the rational mind over our emotional drives, highlighting the importance of understanding and working with, rather than against, the emotional side of our psyche to achieve happiness and well-being. Michael Singer would agree with Haidt as he characterizes ego as the direct result of the Spiritual Self (consciousness) being under the delusion of identification with the body, emotions, and thoughts—the result being "I."[9]

I lean towards Haidt's way of thinking. In my personal experience, my ego tends to want to "make me look good" and "always be right." I've come to realize my authentic self sits underneath this ego. We need to train and tame our elephant to achieve this authenticity.

The Roadmap for Change

These illustrations provide a framework for how the mind works, but they do not define *you*. You are only the observer of these mental processes.

You are not your mind, you are not your body, and you are not your feelings or emotions. You are far more complex than any of it. *You* are pure, conscious energy. You are made of the same energy as every solid object, every star, and everything in the Universe.

The notion that human consciousness could be a fundamental force in the Universe, potentially tied to concepts like vacuum energy (the lowest energy state of a quantum field) or dark energy, ventures into speculative physics, quantum mechanics, and philosophy. However, some intriguing theories and interpretations hint at consciousness being more than just an emergent property of biological processes.

There are a number of scientific certainties that could support consciousness being fundamental to the Universe. They are all based on the science of quantum mechanics. In physics alone, there are many, including the Double-Slit Experiment, which demonstrates the wave-particle duality of light and matter, and the Quantum Eraser Experiments, which demonstrate how decisions made after a quantum event can influence earlier outcomes, challenging our understanding of time and causality. Scan the QR code below to read more about these and other groundbreaking experiments.

Quantum mechanics conditions supporting the possibility of consciousness being more than a byproduct of the brain permeates many sciences, including biology, chemistry, material science, computer science, medicine, astronomy, cosmology, electronics, environmental science, and even philosophy.

My favorite, however, is the quantum biological event of a single cell dividing and organizing into a complex organism. Life itself. This involves the combination of quantum mechanics (at the molecular and atomic levels) and classical biological processes.

At its core, quantum effects influence the molecular interactions and energy transfers that underpin cell division, gene expression, and protein function. These molecular events enable cells to divide, differentiate, and organize into a multicellular organism, following biological processes like mitosis, signaling, and cellular differentiation. While classical biology explains the overarching structure and organization, quantum effects may provide deeper insights into how such remarkable precision and efficiency are achieved at the microscopic level.

In his book *Quantum Body*, Deepak Chopra, M.D., in collaboration with physicist Jack Tuszynski, Ph.D., and endocrinologist Brian Fertig, M.D., delves deeply into the innovative world of quantum science and shows how unlocking its secrets can revolutionize how we live and age—and, ultimately, how we can eradicate disease.[10]

Back to energy. Scientists believe that sixty-eight percent of the Universe is made up of dark energy—something we have yet to detect or identify.[11] Dark energy is the hypothesized background energy of the Universe. It doesn't interact with light or other forms of electromagnetic radiation, making it invisible and detectable only through its effects on the Universe's expansion.

I believe that as we advance in the study of this energy with the aid of AI, we will finally merge ancient wisdom with modern science and ultimately find ourselves. The spiritual energy we are composed of may be the same dark energy that makes up much of the Universe. Throughout history, it has been called many things—Ki, Qi, Chi, Prana, Inner Wind, and many more. In fact, vibration is the process by which energy becomes matter, as Einstein describes in his famous equation $E=mc^2$. The First Law of Thermodynamics, also known as the Law of Energy Conservation, states that energy of any system cannot be created or destroyed, only changed in form. As such, my belief is that our fundamental essence has existed for all time. Now, it exists to observe your mental, emotional, and body self, but when those cease to exist, the truth is that you will continue as it always has.

Almost every religion has a different term for the idea of a formless, universal energy, whether it be the superconscious mind, divinity, the soul, the spiritual self, the higher self, the over self, the conscious receiver, or something entirely different. The energy, by any other name, is still you in your purest form.

Interconnectivity of Self Models

These four types of self—body self, emotional self, mental self, and spiritual self—make up the interconnected models of man. Next, we need to examine how the spiritual self interacts with the body self. We can identify eight levels of interaction measured by heartbeat, breath rate, and average basal metabolic (ABM) rate:

- Death
- Samadhi

- Deep Sleep
- Light and REM Sleep
- Deep Thought or Flow State
- "Monkey Mind"[12]
- Eating
- Running

Death is another way of describing the state when no energy remains active in the body. Any conscious energy once present has left the body and resorted to its original formless state.

Samadhi is a state of extremely low energy achievable only through intense control of mind and body. Very practiced Yogis and other experienced meditators can achieve this state by concentrating all their energy in the superconscious mind, but the body's heart rate, breath rate, and ABM are severely low—barely enough to sustain life. Gamma brainwaves are often associated with this heightened state of consciousness, unity with the Universe, and bliss. We will explore the states of Samadhi much more deeply in Part Three.

The state of Deep Sleep is slightly more active. When we are sleeping deeply, our ABM rate is very slow, and only the subconscious mind is active, working with Delta and Theta waves. But in both Samadhi and Deep Sleep, we observe a powerful phenomenon. Even though energy is subdued, in these states, the body self-heals most effectively. We know this is true from a medical standpoint.

We observe the deep sleep state most often in infants and small children. If you've ever been around a child, they sleep for ten to twelve hours per night, so soundly you can barely wake them up. They need deep sleep to grow and develop, both mentally and physically. The older you get, the less percentage of your night is spent in deep sleep—instead, you cycle between light sleep and REM sleep with perhaps an hour or two of deep sleep.

Light and REM sleep involve a slow ABM rate, but now the subconscious mind is more active, exerting energy toward dreams. We see delta and theta brain waves in these states. Then, in deep thought or flow state, your conscious mind is active—you know you are conscious—but you are so completely focused and locked in that your brain function is practically subconscious.

Next, we have the most common level of brain function: "monkey mind." These are your uncontrolled thoughts and visualizations. Thoughts are even higher vibrations than emotions. In the "monkey mind" state, there is a constant chatter of everything going on in your head, you're frantic, and your brain pattern is beta waves. We can also look at eating and running as two further states where the spiritual, mental, and body selves interact, but these mainly affect the ABM rate rather than mental function. While eating, the ABM rate is medium, and while running, the ABM rate is fast and nearing its upper limit. But these eight states encompass all human energy levels and applications.

There is one final, controversial aspect to understanding interconnectivity, especially regarding our perception of self. We have both internal thoughts and willful thoughts. I'll start by explaining internal thoughts.

Ever since you learned to talk, you have had this voice in your head—your brain has been talking to you. Your inner voice has never changed, either. Think back to when you were little. You've always sounded like yourself, right? Your inner voice never ages and never feels different.

Living in Bliss

No one can control their internal thoughts. Every voice, thought, and picture your brain sends you is entirely predetermined in your subconscious. You don't realize they exist until they hit your consciousness, and you become aware of what your subconscious is making you think.

Your subconscious and unconscious minds are formed by your ancestral genetics. Yes, you are influenced heavily by your parents' genes, but we can go back way further. The genetic changes in your ancestral line as far back as we can go in human history can be found mapped in your DNA. Now, you do have an executive filter for your thoughts. Your prefrontal cortex gives you that buffer against the voice your subconscious sends you straight from your genetic history. That develops sometime before you turn twenty-five.

But here's the controversial part: Willful thoughts—the thoughts you consider to be your free will—are actually still controlled by your subconscious mind. There is no free will, at least, not as we typically understand it. We can show this in an fMRI scan. If I held up an object and asked you what color it was, you might willfully say, "It's blue! No, it's red! No, it's blue!" just to show that you have the free will to say whatever you want.

But the brain imaging would show that your subconscious said blue-red-blue before your mouth and even before your conscious mind did. Regardless of how you perceive your thoughts, your subconscious—your elephant—makes decisions for you, and your consciousness only reflects that choice.

Understandably, this freaks people out. Who would want to live in a world without free will? No one likes the thought of being trapped in an existence as a sort of puppet to the subconscious. But that isn't really the point. We might not have free will, but that doesn't mean we can't change.[IP]

The brain has a remarkable capacity for change. It's called neuroplasticity. This ability allows it to reorganize and form new neural connections. We can create new neural pathways in response to new experiences, injuries, and information. This means we can adapt and recover in the realm of cognitive development. By giving ourselves new experiences, we remap our brains, changing how our subconscious makes choices.

Now, we know genes are set in stone. Your parents and your history have established your genetic identity. That cannot change. However, with recent studies in epigenetics, we have discovered a capability to change gene expression by turning genes on or off. Some are controlled by time, some by environment, and some by you. Our behaviors and mental states can lead to changes at the genetic level through epigenetic mechanisms. The body "remembers" certain environmental influences via chemical tags on DNA (e.g., methylation), which can turn genes on or off. Internally, the spiritual you possesses the ability to remap its brain, its subconscious, and its genetics. We will dive deeper into epigenetics and neuroplasticity in the next chapter.

Epigenetics is perhaps why the placebo effect works. The placebo effect occurs when a person experiences real physiological or psychological improvements after receiving a treatment that has no therapeutic value, like a sugar pill. The belief in the treatment's efficacy triggers a complex set of biological responses, including changes in brain activity, hormone levels, and immune function.

Said another way, something can work for you because you believe it's working for you. When people test a new drug, the placebo effect can vary widely, ranging from twenty to fifty percent depending on the condition and trial design. The level of improvement required above placebo depends on the condition, but in areas like depression and pain, ten to twenty percent greater efficacy over placebo is often a benchmark.

So, no, you don't have free will. Your thoughts and decisions are predetermined in your subconscious and unconscious. But we have a more powerful capacity than just thinking willfully. We can go straight to the source, reshaping ourselves at the subconscious and genetic levels.

If we can control our mind to truly believe what we believe, we are ultimately powerful. And why wouldn't we be? You are your higher self. That energy that is you is the energy of the Universe. As you learn to harness this power and establish yourself in your spiritual self, there is nothing you can't do for the temporary time you are in your body.

If you are curious about mind-body interconnectivity, scan the QR code below to access additional resources.

PART 2

Balancing Body, Mind, and Spirit

To keep the body in good health is a duty… otherwise we shall not be able to keep our mind strong and clear. Peace comes from within. Do not seek it without.

—Buddha

3

Healing the Body

The journey to healing begins with a deep desire to transform, which, unfortunately, is often sparked by pain, illness, or an unfulfilled longing to live more fully. In my life, the suffering has never been great, but it is always a matter of degree. The higher the level of suffering, the greater the chance you either collapse and it destroys you or you find a bottom and bounce back.

Healing is never just about alleviating discomfort and returning to neutral. It's about building vitality, resilience, and alignment between body, mind, and spirit until you are living with more creativity, purpose, and joy than ever before. A healthy body is the foundation it all starts with. At its core, the quest for physical healing is about rediscovering the innate wisdom of the body and committing to its care and growth. I am a big advocate of stating your point up front. So, here it is. Do more good than bad to your body.[IP] Do more to your body to promote health and longevity than the bad things we inevitably do. The concept is simple to understand but hard to put into regular practice.

I've already discussed the suffering it took to get me to the point of change. At my moment of self-inspection, when I was forty-three, my decision to do something about it was born.

> **The path to healing unfolds through the deliberate flow of commitment, learning, and action, with each phase offering critical steps toward transformation.**

Commitment, Learning, and Action

Through all my learning, I needed practical answers to one question: What is the process flow for self-improvement? The path to healing unfolds through the deliberate flow of commitment, learning, and action, with each phase offering critical steps toward transformation.

Commit

My commitment began with a deep acknowledgment of my need for change. This involved taking a personal inventory to identify all my unhealthy habits and patterns, whether they stemmed from physical, mental, or emotional sources.

For me, it was all three. I had poor eating habits and portion control, a contentment with being identified as a big, powerful man, and an inferiority complex, leading me to eat for comfort.

The first time I lost weight, I set specific, achievable goals. This meant following an Atkins diet for over a year. I dropped

Healing the Body

to a low of 259 pounds and was able to stay around 270 for most of the next six years, or so. During this time, I didn't just improve my diet; I took up tennis and remained physically active. I had also started meditating periodically to manage stress, but I didn't clearly understand what I was doing.

To this point, I never lost enough weight that I ever got off any medications, which by this time included Metformin and Trulicity for my diabetes, various blood pressure medications, and a statin for cholesterol. On top of it all, stressful events like a failing marriage and the loss of my job triggered an autoimmune disorder, which manifested as a form of systemic arthritis and psoriasis combined. For that, I was taking a biologic to reduce inflammation as well as various sexual performance drugs.

I wish I had made myself more accountable during this time, either by writing down my intentions or clearly stating them to loved ones to solidify them as a contract with myself. I now understand that committing yourself is far more deliberate than simply making a decision. Where there is commitment, there is investment and a fundamental alteration of thought patterns. I would love to remind my past self to cultivate a belief in the body's innate capacity to heal and that progress is not about perfection but about consistent effort over time.[IP]

After my second marriage to Maureen and the birth of our first daughter, Emilia, both in 2018, I began to gain weight once again. By the time COVID struck in 2020, I weighed 295 pounds.

I caught COVID fairly early on, and while I was never hospitalized overnight, I did get pneumonia. It scared me and led me to seek out the services of Princeton Longevity Center for a comprehensive analysis of my health. I'll never forget the dialogue. After what seemed like an interminable amount of time reviewing my chart, the doctor closed it, laid it on the table in front of him, looked me dead in the eye, and said, "Pete, you know there are no fat old people!"

I was floored at his bluntness. He continued, "I don't know why you would want to be a fat person, but I see a history here of gaining and losing weight. If I were you, I would get weight loss surgery, and I would talk to a psychiatrist." By reminding me that weight gain was a product of life choices, he prompted me to consider my decisions and their long-term consequences.

Learn

Learning was the next step in the journey. I needed to equip myself with the knowledge and tools needed for the journey. The best way to do this is to find the experts. Who are the masters in the area of self-improvement you have committed to? Once you identify and learn about them, find out who taught them.

General Stanley McChrystal counsels that you should always have a mentor above you, further along in the process, but also a mentor below you with perhaps less experience but still plenty of wisdom.[13] It is also essential to have peers who mentor at your level, as they do the same things you do but with different strengths.

In any process of self-improvement, you also need an accountability guide. This person can be one or all of your mentors, a peer, or anyone you trust enough to be genuine and honest with one hundred percent of the time.

While I never did see a psychiatrist, I did read and met doctors to discuss my weight loss surgery options. I engaged with friends and others who had undergone various bariatric surgeries as well. Besides this, I began identifying trusted sources of information, such as healthcare professionals, holistic practitioners, and evidence-based wellness programs.

I diversified my learning by exploring different schools of thought, including integrative medicine, ancient healing traditions, and modern technological advances. I read incessantly about others who had faced similar health challenges. I researched various wellness apps, podcasts, and books to tailor my goals and to gain insights and strategies. In the end, I was well-equipped to take my next steps.

Do

Transformation takes root in action, where intention meets implementation. Despite the somewhat dismaying long-term statistics around bariatric surgery, I decided to have a Sleeve Gastrectomy. About twenty to twenty-five percent of patients regain a significant portion of lost weight within five to ten years, often linked to lifestyle factors, behavioral patterns, or physiological adaptations.[14][15][16]

Gastric bypass and sleeve gastrectomy result in Type 2 diabetes remission in up to sixty to eighty percent of cases initially, with some decline over time.[17][18][19] That said, it remains the best decision I ever made for my health. My all-time low was 206 pounds, but a good portion of that resulted from a loss of lean muscle and fat. I use a smart scale to track my performance on a regular basis against a series of goals.

Description	Start	Initial Goal	2025
Weight	358 / 295 Lbs.	220 Lbs.	199 Lbs.
Total Body Fat	23.5%	15.0%	14.7%
Visceral Fat	17.5 Lbs.	11 Lbs.	8 Lbs.

| Muscle Mass | 218 Lbs. (73.9%) | 165 Lbs. (75.0%) | 161 Lbs. (81.0%) |
| Medications | 8 | 0 | 3* |

* I am actively choosing to stay on Metformin, Testosterone, and a low-dose statin

By integrating commitment, learning, and action into your approach, you create a self-sustaining cycle of healthy improvement. This framework not only enhances your capacity to heal but also instills resilience, preparing you to face future challenges with strength and clarity.

Healthspan Versus Lifespan

When you undertake a transformation of your body, all progress is beneficial. But the next questions you need to ask yourself pertain to longevity:

- Will these interventions extend my lifespan?
- If I am living longer, what percentage of my years will be spent in good health?
- Is there a way for my health habits to improve my healthspan indefinitely?

Lifespan refers to the total years one lives, while healthspan measures the period of life spent in good health. As we progress into the future with new technologies, healing will be able to bridge this gap by enhancing both the length and quality of life.

Ray Kurzweil, a renowned inventor, futurist, and author known for his groundbreaking work in technology and predictions about the future of humanity, is known for discussing the concept of "longevity escape velocity," which refers to the idea that advancements in medicine and technology will eventually allow us to extend human life faster than we age, effectively halting the aging process over time.[20]

Artificial intelligence (AI) will play an increasingly significant role in this area, offering innovations like personalized medicine, early disease detection, robotic precision in treatments, and real-time behavioral feedback through wearables. AI is also accelerating longevity research, enabling breakthroughs in anti-aging and regenerative therapies.

At an Abundance360 conference I attended in 2023, Hans Keirstead, Ph.D., an internationally known stem cell expert leading therapy development for cancer, immune disorders, motor neuron diseases, spinal cord injury and retinal diseases, walked on stage and proudly proclaimed, "Live the next ten to twenty years as healthfully as you can, and don't die of something stupid, because within thirty years, science and technology will have solved all major diseases, including aging, which is just another disease."

In keeping with this theme, at the same conference, David Sinclair, A.O., Ph.D., a tenured Professor in the Genetics Department at Harvard Medical School, stated, "There is no biological limit to human life… of course there isn't… it's ninety-nine percent a software problem." Nature shows us that incredible longevity is not a hardware problem: The bowhead whale may be the longest-lived mammal, with the ability to reach an age of more than 200 years.[21] Greenland sharks have the longest lifespan of any known vertebrate, estimated to be between 250 and 500 years.[22] The human potential for long life can be maximized with care. The latest evidence suggests that approximately a quarter of the variation in human lifespan is caused by genetic differences between individuals.[23] [24] The rest is influenced by epigenetic and environmental factors.

How to Live Healthy, Longer

Dan Buettner's study of the world's Blue Zones—regions where people live exceptionally long and healthy lives—offers invaluable insights on how to live healthy, longer. In his Netflix docuseries *Live to 100: Secrets of the Blue Zones*, Buettner explores regions renowned for their inhabitants' exceptional longevity and vitality.[25] He highlights ten practices common to all the locations as the root of their reputation:

1. Regular physical activity
2. Purpose-driven life
3. Stress-reducing rituals
4. Limiting overeating
5. Whole-food plant-based diets
6. Moderate alcohol intake
7. Participation in a faith-based or spiritual community
8. Emphasis on family and care for elders
9. Like-minded community
10. Strong mental and social activity

These practices emphasize the importance of a lifestyle that integrates physical, emotional, and communal well-being. For more information on the Blue Zones, the practices that can extend your health span, and the experts in longevity, scan the QR code below.

I think Dan Sullivan, Co-Founder and President of Strategic Coach® and the world's foremost expert on entrepreneurship in action, says it best: "A key to longevity is having a future that is bigger than your past."[26] So much of my bigger future has come from numbers nine and ten of Buettner's list: a strong community. Put yourself out there. You will live happier and longer.

Longevity Mindset

A key aspect of my longevity practices is cultivating and sustaining a Longevity Mindset, heavily inspired by Peter Diamandis' books and personal guidance. Many of the concepts in this chapter first appeared in his book, *Longevity*, published in 2023.[27] This mindset stems from a belief in the power of science to extend our health span by decades.

Adopting a Longevity Mindset means embracing the role of "CEO of your own health" and shifting your perspective to see life not as short but as something you can actively extend and optimize.

Your lifespan and healthspan are influenced by multiple factors: birthplace, genetics, lifestyle choices, and most importantly, your mindset. Contrary to popular belief, longevity isn't predetermined by your genetic inheritance.

In fact, a 2018 study of 54 million individuals found that genetics account for only about 7 percent of lifespan variation.[28] Other estimates suggest up to 30 percent, meaning that lifestyle choices and environment control at least 70 percent of how long and well you live. This puts the power firmly in your hands to shape your healthspan.

According to Peter Diamandis, there are several key areas to focus on when cultivating your Longevity Mindset:[29]

1. **Belief.** Your expectations about your lifespan shape your actions. Do you see life as short and hope to make it to 75 or 80? Or do you aim to live vibrantly beyond 100, redefining aging as a manageable, even reversible condition? A few years ago, I believed I would be lucky to live into my 80s, but with what I've learned, I fervently believe I will live well into my hundreds and be healthfully active right up to the end.

2. **Media Consumption.** The information you absorb influences your mindset. Are you consuming negative or limiting content, or are you engaging with resources that inspire longevity? Just like the old adage, "you are what you eat," I believe it's just as true to say, "you are what you read and listen to."

3. **Community.** The people you surround yourself with have an immense impact. Are you part of a supportive, optimistic community that values health and longevity? Sharing best practices and encouraging

each other can significantly shape your actions. I am truly blessed to be accepted into so many diverse yet like-minded communities and groups. Diversity is indeed the "spice of life." This is akin to the fact that my three daughters will, statistically speaking, live longer because of their genetic diversity—testing reveals they have no less than eleven different lineages as part of their genetic makeup.

4. **Sleep.** Sleep is a cornerstone of health. Aim for at least eight hours each night, as experts like Dr. Matthew Walker recommended in *Why We Sleep*.[30] He recommends a regular bedtime, darkness, coolness, no caffeine after 12 p.m., no alcohol or sugar near bedtime, no food after 7 p.m., having a wind down routine, and 300-400 mg of Ashwagandha, 3–4 g of Glycine, and 1–3 mg of Melatonin if needed. Quality rest is not negotiable if you want to optimize your healthspan.

5. **Diet.** Your diet profoundly impacts your body. Are you eating mindlessly, indulging in sugars and processed foods? Or have you adopted a deliberate, healthful diet rich in whole foods, plants, and sufficient protein to build muscle and support longevity?

6. **Exercise.** Regular exercise, especially strength and high-intensity interval training, is critical for increasing muscle mass and promoting longevity. Evaluate your routine—are you sedentary or achieving consistent activity and strength-building exercises? Remember, this doesn't mean you have to work out for hours every day. Per Dan Buettner's findings discussed earlier, simply getting up and moving

regularly has contributed to the longevity of some of the oldest people alive.

7. **Annual Health Diagnostics.** Don't leave your health to chance. Leverage modern diagnostic technologies to detect potential issues early, when they're easiest to address.

Your mindset, particularly having something meaningful to live for, plays a crucial role in longevity. History offers a striking example of this principle. Founding Fathers Thomas Jefferson and John Adams willed themselves to live to see the fiftieth anniversary of the Declaration of Independence. Both surpassed the average life expectancy of their time, passing away on the exact date of the anniversary in 1826, driven by their strong sense of purpose.

Set a bold target for your health span—whether it's 100, 120, or even more—and program this goal into your mindset. Share your aspirations with conviction, inspiring those around you to think differently about longevity.

Optimism matters. A long-term study published in *Proceedings of the National Academy of Sciences* found that optimistic individuals live up to fifteen percent longer than pessimists.[31] With so many tools and opportunities at your disposal today, there's every reason to embrace the potential for an extended, vibrant life.

Ultimately, the goal is to thrive in every dimension—body, mind, and spirit—living a life of energy, connection, and purpose in harmony with the body's innate potential. We can move beyond simply adding years to our lives. Instead, we can focus on adding life to our years—living fully, vibrantly, and healthily, no matter our age.

If you are curious about more specific practices you can employ to heal your body, scan the QR code below. I have compiled some of my research and experiences into actionable strategies. Your health is your greatest asset. Start today to take control, reshape your mindset, and unlock the extraordinary possibilities for a longer, healthier future.

4

Healing the Mind

As stated in the first chapter, I began this journey on the premise that healing the mind started with an understanding of happiness. Turns out it's a lot more. Let me start with the answer up front again: Fill your mind with more good thoughts, feelings, and emotions than bad ones, and that's the life you will experience.[IP] As previously stated, this is obvious but difficult to put into daily practice.

I wish I could say my journey to mental healing was as easy as following a preplanned process. Life would be grand indeed if I could cast a vision for myself that automatically filtered down to the mundane and fixed everything.

What I can say, however, is that vision helped me to take stock of where I was. When I hit a low, I looked backward, up into my life, and reflected on how I got to my current state. Even just identifying poor decisions in my past helped me to see what decisions I did not want my future to include.

I built a framework for how I wanted to live. I have since evolved my original framework to one introduced to me by Jay Rifenbary in his Blueprint for Character.[32] His five elements are essential to how I want to be remembered and are my goals in the transformation of my mind.

1. **Core values.** What do you stand for and believe in at the expense of anything and everything else? I identified and established my values and will discuss them in depth later.

2. **Accountability.** I knew I needed to concentrate on reasons for doing things rather than excuses. An excuse is when the same—often poor—reason becomes a habit. It is my choice to determine how I behave. I will accept no excuses from anyone, especially myself. Your core values can help hold you accountable to these declarations.

3. **Personal Honesty.** Needs and fears are the foundation of decision-making but are also the hardest to come to terms with. I forced myself to honestly identify what I was afraid to do, compared it to what I needed to do, and used that discrepancy as the foundation for my decisions.

4. **Integrity.** Integrity is the consistency of behavior, mindset, systems, and habits, all rooted in a foundation of morality. The best way to assess that morality is to take a look at how you treat another human being.

5. **Leadership.** I have always been a leader in one way or another, so this one was an easy addition to this list. The difficult part is breaking down what it takes

to be a good leader. Authenticity in leadership takes a combination of vulnerability, humility, and transparency, while professionalism in leadership really just requires emotional intelligence, resilience, and patience.

Your own blueprint can borrow significantly from these five elements, but feel free to personalize it with the elements of life you most want to be remembered for.

Mental Well-Being

The well-being of the mind has ties to the other two aspects of self: body and spirit. The mind is intrinsically linked to the quantum field just as the body is. We're always going to cross back into healing the body and forward to the spirit.

We can start with the superficial portion of healing the mind, though. Haidt proposes three components to well-being: physical, psychological, and social.[33]

Physical well-being is enhanced by everything I discussed in the previous chapter. Exercise, eating right, and other interventions all contribute to your body's health. But any physical concern has immediate crossover into the mental plane. Mental health issues surround exercise, eating, community, interpersonal interactions, and anything else you might imagine.

We're already well into the second piece: mental well-being. Just like physical exercise, maintaining mental capabilities is contingent upon overcoming the tendency to not use what you have been given. It's the use it or lose it principle. For example, muscle fitness deteriorates much more quickly than you might think. In studies where athletes are confined to bed rest, researchers found that the lack of physical activity significantly decreases endurance exercise performance within as little as three days.[34] Another study shows that the ratio of loss in muscle strength is highest after only five days.[35]

If you aren't using it, you are losing it. Luckily, our bodies and minds are resilient, so even if there is some loss in physical or mental well-being, we can snap back with a little concentrated effort. Granted, we lose this resilience as we age, so the younger we are, the more enthusiastically our bodies snap back.

I recently developed tinnitus, and the persistent ringing has been intensely annoying. My doctor told me that mild hearing loss was causing it. The intriguing part about this discovery, though, is how my brain no longer receives certain signals from my ears because of the hearing loss, so it then interjects its own signal to fill the void, which is interpreted as ringing.

My doctor suggested hearing aids, not because my hearing loss has affected me—I wouldn't have noticed it without the side effect of tinnitus—but because if the hearing aids help my brain receive the missing signal again, it will shut off the ringing frequency. Sure enough, that is exactly what happened.

Here's my aha moment: I began researching deafness and discovered that individuals with moderate to severe hearing loss have a sixty-one percent higher prevalence of dementia compared to those with normal hearing.[36] It fits beautifully into the use it or lose it principle. Hearing and seeing are both highly energetic mental processes. If your brain is no longer receiving input from one of those sources, it is no longer utilizing a large allotment of its capacity. It then loses its capacity for cognitive ability.

We need to do whatever we can to stay mentally active in order to keep our brains thriving as we get older. Just like lifting weights enhances our physical well-being, maintaining good mental health and hygiene is crucial to maintaining cognitive ability.

The third component of well-being is psychological: how much happiness is in your life? Jonathan Haidt represents his Happiness Hypothesis as an equation:[37]

$$H = S + C + V$$

S stands for your happiness set point, C is your living conditions, and V is your voluntary actions.

The set point is our default happiness level, which is incredibly difficult to change. Living conditions are also tricky because they are only partially under our control. Where, when, and to whom you are born all affect your living conditions, whether you like it or not. You can adjust these factors later in life, but it takes great effort.

The one happiness contributor we have uninhibited control of is our voluntary acts. This is where your strengths or "superpowers" come into play. Your superpowers are your instinctive strengths—those things that give you great happiness because they are easy for you to do. They come naturally to you. You didn't have to learn them or train them.

I'm going to add a fourth component: awe.

I like Haidt's equation, but I would add two factors. The first is expectation. Mo Gawdat, a previous chief business officer at Google X, lost a child at one point in his life and had to bring himself back from the brink. One of his conclusions was that our expectations drive us to not be happy.

If we have expectations, fears, ego, or preconceived notions about what happiness is, then we're going to be unhappy because life is unpredictable.

The other component I will add is awe. When we seek experiences of awe regularly, our happiness quotient soars.

With that in mind, here is my version of the happiness equation:

$$H = S + C + V + A - E^{IP}$$

A is awe, and E is expectations. We have control over those as well as our voluntary acts. Let's review a few techniques for eliminating expectations and increasing awe.

Eliminating Expectation

I love a quote attributed to Bruce Lee: "I'm not in this world to live up to your expectations, and you're not in this world to live up to mine."[38] Expectation is almost synonymous with the perception of control. Control, of course, is an illusion. We don't have control over external circumstances. A good way to get rid of the perception is to focus on what we can control, which is our reaction to external events.

A second technique is to practice radical acceptance and accept life as an immutable reality. This promotes detachment as you let go of outcomes and focus on effort. The only way to change reality is through your own struggle. It also promotes humility as you ask yourself, "How can I give back?" and "How can I contribute to the greater good in this situation?"

A third method would be disengaging from social validation. External influences like social media and societal standards excel at jacking up unhealthy expectations for what life should be like.

Finally, overcome your fear. Fear is nothing more than an imagined future or perceived threat. It's an expectation of harm that can only undermine your happiness. It also helps to develop resilience to fear by building confidence in your ability to adapt. Recognize there have been times where you've overcome fear in your life. Practice reminding yourself of those moments. Reframe failures and risks as challenges and opportunities to learn from rather than threats to avoid.

In addition to the above three techniques, I have identified seven expectations we all have that utterly drain our peace and joy:

1. Stop expecting everyone to agree with you (stay true to your purpose).
2. Stop expecting people to show you more respect than you show yourself.
3. Stop expecting everyone to like you.
4. Stop expecting people to perfectly align with your idea of who they are.
5. Stop expecting everyone to know or understand what you are thinking.
6. Stop expecting seemingly strong people to be perfect.
7. Stop expecting people you know to suddenly change.

All these things will work towards reducing your expectations in general and thus boosting your happiness and mental well-being.

Awe

In the winter of 2023, freelance writer Ashley Stimpson wrote an outstanding article titled "Awestruck," published in *Johns Hopkins Magazine*.[39] Ever since reading it, I've reflected on my own life and realized the importance of seeking out little doses of awe every day.

Johns Hopkins researchers are pioneering the study of awe, a powerful and transformative emotion, by integrating virtual reality (VR) and psychedelic research. Awe is that profound sensation we experience when confronted with something vast and extraordinary—whether a stunning sunset, a grand symphony, or the birth of a child. It momentarily shifts our perception, diminishes our sense of self, and can even alter our experience of time. Now, scientists are uncovering its measurable effects on mental health and exploring ways to harness it for therapeutic benefits.

Awe has long been recognized in philosophy and psychology by thinkers like Immanuel Kant, Edmund Burke, and Charles Darwin. However, until recently, there was no standardized way to scientifically measure awe. Early studies simply asked participants if they felt awe, but definitions varied. In response, Johns Hopkins researcher David Yaden and his team developed the Awe Experience Scale, a thirty-item questionnaire designed to quantify the emotion.[40] They identified six key characteristics of awe:

1. Self-diminishment: Feeling small in the face of something vast

2. Time alteration: A perception of time slowing or standing still

3. Physical sensations: Goosebumps, chills, or a dropped jaw

4. Connectedness: A deep sense of unity with others and the Universe

5. Vastness: The feeling of encountering something grand or overwhelming

6. Cognitive accommodation: Struggling to process the immensity of an experience

To test their framework, Yaden and his team asked over 1,100 participants to describe awe-inspiring moments, ranging from encounters with nature to witnessing acts of profound human achievement. The findings confirmed that awe is a distinct and universal emotion, one that shapes our perception of the world and our place in it.

Modern research suggests that experiencing awe reduces stress, depression, and anxiety while enhancing overall well-being.[41] Studies show that individuals who regularly experience awe report higher life satisfaction, lower levels of inflammation, and even improved social behavior.[42] One experiment revealed that people who stared at towering eucalyptus trees were more likely to help a stranger afterward, highlighting awe's ability to increase empathy and altruism.[43]

While scientific breakthroughs may soon bring engineered awe experiences, researchers emphasize that awe is already within our reach. Berkeley psychologist Dacher Keltner, who helped shape modern awe research, found that most people experience awe multiple times per week—whether through nature, music, art, spirituality, or witnessing acts of moral beauty.

Keltner's research identified eight "wonders" of life that commonly evoke awe:

1. Moral beauty: Witnessing acts of kindness and courage

2. Nature: Majestic landscapes, towering mountains, or a starry sky

3. Collective movement: Watching synchronized dance or sports

4. Music: Hearing a breathtaking symphony or song

5. Art: Masterpieces that move the soul

6. Spirituality: Moments of deep transcendence or faith

7. Big ideas: Discovering profound scientific or philosophical truths

8. Mortality: Encounters with life, death, and the fleeting nature of existence[44]

Incorporating awe into daily life is not only possible but also transformative. Whether it's watching a sunrise, reading a mind-expanding book, or witnessing human resilience, awe reminds us of life's grandeur.

I've since realized my youth was filled with moments of awe[IP], which is probably why I am able to relatively easily invoke an internal state of awe in my daily meditation routine. I have learned that awe is not just an emotion; it is a gateway to a higher state of being. It humbles us, expands our awareness, and dissolves the barriers between self and world. In moments of awe, we touch the infinite, experiencing life as something vast, interconnected, and sacred.

In an age where we are increasingly caught up in the minutiae of daily life, awe pulls us out of our smallness and into the grandeur of existence. It reminds us that beyond our worries, beyond our ambitions, beyond even our own identities, lies something far greater, timeless, and beautifully unknowable.

I suggest that every day we step outside, look up at the stars, lose ourselves in a piece of music, or stand in silent reverence before a work of art. The sublime is always within reach. Awe is waiting.

5

Discover Your Superpowers

Do What You Do Best

If the concept of having superpowers seems like it belongs in comic books, don't worry. All it takes is a little reflection to find your own.

Start by investigating your youth. What are the most joyful times you remember from your childhood? What stories are the easiest to recall from when you were young? As you relive those moments, do any repeated themes stand out? In times of idleness, your brain looked for happiness in those stories and memories, and eventually, they became your default mode network. Whether you knew it or not, you built an affinity toward doing those couple of things, and they became your superpowers.

Happiness is endemic to all of us—we just need to discover our strengths.[IP] And if we do voluntary acts on a regular basis that are aligned with our superpowers, we give ourselves the gift of happiness in the present. Every day I spend operating in my superpowers, I am increasing my happiness quotient.

I have five superpowers, so I don't necessarily engage with each one every day. But no matter what I'm doing, I make sure I employ one of them so that it always contributes to my greater happiness. Your superpowers are your own, and you will have to embark on your own journey to discover yours, but I hope the following descriptions of my superpowers give you a good idea of where to start.

> **Happiness is endemic to all of us— we just need to discover our strengths.[IP]**

The Power of Continuous Learning and Integrating

My first and most fervent superpower is learning. I am a lifelong learner, perpetually finding new areas to research. Every day, I give myself the gift of learning by talking to people, reading books, listening to podcasts, and researching the masters and the non-experts alike. Every encounter exposes me to new information and new modes of thinking. It helps me to make sure I am not closed off to anything just because I might be biased toward one frame of thought.

For me, learning is never about how much I know, and it's especially not about lording my knowledge over others. Every time I learn something new, it is primarily a discovery of all the things I don't know. A new world of possibility opens up with every new piece of information.

When I engage in voluntary acts of learning, it raises the happiness quotient for my whole life. This pursuit overflows into how I engage with others. Most of the companies I have created are intentionally organized as learning-based organizations, meaning that perpetual learning is a core value of the company.

Mastering Concentration and Focus

My second superpower is concentration and focus. I've been an avid meditator for many years. I rarely miss my daily meditations, and I use different types of meditations throughout the day, from small moments of breathful mindfulness all the way to deep spiritual meditation. So I give myself the gift of deep concentration and deep focus, and it, too, drives up my happiness and awe quotient.

Visionary and Futurist Thinking

My superpower of being a visionary enables my roles as a dad and a CEO. A CEO has four jobs:

- Be a visionary (you can alternatively be the integrator, but you cannot be both)
- Be captain of the cash flow
- Be a chief coach, mentor, and motivator
- Be the architect of culture

So my first job as CEO is to have a vision of the future. I must anticipate what's going to happen in the world so I can lead the company through obstacles. Meditation actually flows into my capacity as a visionary. When I meditate, I often receive great insights along with a clear and unfettered picture of what the future could be. What I see is not absolutely written in stone, but it gives me a clear and concise picture of the future, which gives me purpose, which then gives me direction.

I give myself that gift of vision by thinking about the vision of the future every day, and you can see how my strengths all correlate to one another.

Teaching, Coaching, and Motivating Through Storytelling

Jay Rifenbarry said, "We teach best in life what we want to learn the most." Learning is one of my strongest inclinations, and teaching naturally flows out of it. I'm a coach, a mentor, a CEO, a dad to my older son and three little girls, and I'm a grandfather too. When I give myself the gift of coaching and mentoring through any and all of these capacities, I thrive.

I stopped coaching early in my career, and as soon as I did, I intrinsically felt a loss in my life. Eventually, I realized that loss was because it was one of my superpowers feeding my happiness quotient. When it was gone, I didn't have the joy to replace it, and anxiety rushed in to fill the gap.

I haven't gone back to coaching completely, but now I know how to employ my mentoring superpower in ways that fill the void. I've engrossed myself as a mentor by joining communities like Abundance360, writing a book, and interacting with others in new ways.

Simplifying Life as a Facilitator

Facilitating is key as a business leader. Everything you do is to make life easier for yourself, your clients, your employees, and your loved ones. When I go through personal difficulty, I always look for ways to simplify and universalize the lessons I learn so they benefit not only me but all those around me as well. It's like putting up a circus tent. Once that center pole goes up, it props up the rest of the tent with it. You are the tent pole in your life—if you elevate yourself, all those around you are elevated as well.

That's why I love simplifying life as a facilitator and galvanizer. One reason I am writing this book is to take the big, frightening truths of the world I am learning about and clarify them so everyone can benefit. These ideas—the mind-body connection, the quantum field—are not well-known, especially in the Western world of modern medicine and the objective reality of Newtonian physics. It gives me energy to facilitate knowledge of these things through the form of this book.

These five superpowers have been instrumental in my happiness. I can consistently raise the most controllable portion of the psychological well-being quotient—voluntary acts—by just doing the things I love. You will be amazed by how free you feel when you identify your superpowers and start to give them to yourself as daily gifts.

6

Live Your Core Values

Presence, Purpose, and Prosperity[IP]

Once you make it a habit of filling your life with superpower-fueled happiness, you will notice a difference in your mental well-being. To make sure your progress is sustainable, you will have to continue the thought process constantly to stave off the failure of information in the quantum field. The quantum field is the perfect place of knowledge. I am a quantum body—one with the ability to hold knowledge and process information. But I need to continue to build mental muscle in order for it to maintain health through the ups and downs of life. What will you hold onto to steady yourself? Your core values.

In creating core values, you must answer the question, "What is it that I want to become, and how do I want to be represented?" The answer forms your core values, but they can change throughout your life. I have three core values to guide and ground my every action:

- Presence[IP]
- Purpose
- Prosperity[IP]

If your core values stabilize you, then mindsets move you forward. I have eight mindsets to govern my actions, and each is shaped by my core values:

- Mindfulness
- Humility
- Curiosity
- Abundance
- Massively Transformative Purpose (MTP)
- Exponential Thinking
- Taking "Moonshots"
- Gratitude

Whenever I find myself not being in alignment with my superpowers, core values, and mindset, I ask myself, "Am I wilfully choosing this alternate path, or am I just wasting time?" The answer results in an adjustment to my thinking or puts me back on track—either way, it's a good thing. As I go through each core value in detail, I will explain how each works in conjunction with my mindset to produce applications for everyday life.

Presence

A little-known German philosopher, known as Meister Eckhart, claimed, "I have often said that God is creating the entire Universe fully and totally in this present now. Everything God creates, he creates 'now' all at once."

I find this conclusion fascinating because while he is a mystic, Deepak Chopra says essentially the same thing in his new book, *Quantum Body*.[45] He explains the quantum field as identical to the idea of everything being *now*. The smallest details conform to the big picture. We are each a quantum body of intelligence and have some degree of control over a quantum field of perfect information.

Remember how I said the Universe is not just matter and energy, but it's also information? That universal knowledge, as it relates to us, is our quantum body. It takes perfect intelligence to do the millions of metabolic cellular processes that happen to us every day. The perfection only breaks down when it encounters the environment we expose ourselves to and our imperfect DNA. From there, we grow into imperfect humans with imperfect childhoods and, ultimately, an imperfect prefrontal cortex.

That imperfection is why we need to heal the body, mind, and spirit in the first place. Well-being breaks down whenever there is a failure in intelligence, but well-being is strengthened whenever intelligence flows naturally.

Being a dad to three young girls, I came upon this quote from, of all places, Master Oogway from *Kung Fu Panda*, but it captures my sentiment perfectly: "The past is history. The future is a mystery. Today [Now] is a gift, and that's why they call it the present."[46]

Presence is my first core value because I acknowledge this truth. I believe all humanity must learn how to live in the present because the now is where all creation resides. Every time we dwell in the past or the future, we live in what Buddha called a world of suffering.

In the end, I have discovered that presence is the path to the center of universal knowledge—of being. Presence is the connection point between the center of "self" and the oneness of all.

Mindset Connection

Mindfulness directly enhances presence by promoting awareness and engagement in the current moment. It helps you focus on the here and now.

Humility keeps you open to learning from each moment. It encourages genuine interactions and attentiveness to others.

Curiosity drives you to explore and fully experience the present moment. It keeps you engaged and interested in your immediate environment.

An **abundance** mindset allows you to appreciate and make the most of the present moment. It fosters gratitude and a positive outlook.

Having an **MTP** provides a strong sense of direction and focus, allowing you to be fully present in actions that align with your broader mission.

Exponential thinking requires a deep understanding of current capabilities and trends, grounding you in the present while planning for the future.

Pursuing **moonshots** keeps you engaged and focused on ambitious goals but requires being attuned to current possibilities and resources.

Gratitude fosters a deep appreciation for the current moment and the people in it. It helps you focus on the positive aspects of the present, enhancing your sense of fulfillment.

Purpose

My next core value is purpose. Purpose is that which we want to be known for. It gives us direction to shape our lives and actions. Moonshots are an excellent example of living with purpose. A moonshot is something tactical to strive for, like writing a book or owning a company. The direction of every company I've started and every investment I have made is related to my desire to improve the world during the time of AI—the most influential technological advancement we have ever seen. I want to make AI approachable. That's one of my moonshots.

Another is to achieve enlightenment—a balanced existence of body, mind, and spirit and become fully centered in my higher self. I want to elevate the collective consciousness with me by fostering a world where every individual can realize their highest potential and live in harmony. This book is a step toward achieving that.

If you want to learn more about my moonshots, visit PeteSacco.com or scan the QR code below.

The other strategy for emphasizing purpose in your life is putting your Massively Transformative Purpose (MTP) into words. My MTP is to inspire and accelerate mankind's transition to a world where every digital interaction is rooted in transparency and trust, empowering individuals, leaders, and communities through decentralized technology, open AI, and robust digital asset security.

Mindset Connection

Mindfulness allows for deeper introspection, helping you stay aligned with your core purpose. It enables you to make conscious decisions that reflect your mission and values.

Humility ensures that you remain open to feedback and new perspectives, helping you stay true to your purpose and continuously improve.

Curiosity fuels the pursuit of knowledge and understanding. It helps you discover new paths and refine your mission.

Believing in **abundance** helps you pursue your purpose without fear of scarcity. It encourages generosity and sharing.

An **MTP** embodies your core value of purpose by driving you towards significant and meaningful goals. It provides a clear and compelling vision for your efforts.

Exponential thinking aligns with your visionary and futurist strengths, helping you envision and work toward transformative goals.

Moonshots are inherently aligned with a purpose-driven mindset, as they aim for transformative and meaningful impact.

Gratitude promotes a positive and appreciative outlook on your journey and achievements. It helps you recognize the value in your efforts and stay motivated.

Prosperity

Finally, we come to the core value of prosperity. It is my goal in life to live and improve myself, not out of egoistic motivations but out of selflessness.

Buddha said that the secrets to life are threefold: one, enlightenment comes when you realize living in the past or the future is a life of suffering; two, life is ever-changing; and three, live selflessly.

So, to me, prosperity is learning to live selflessly in servitude to others, with gratitude for all things. Prosperity flows from these. Well-being is prosperity, as are wealth and relationships. But it is our job to improve ourselves so that we can contribute to the prosperity of the collective consciousness of the Universe.

Selflessness is our gift to the Universe.[IP]

Mindset Connection

A **mindful** approach helps you manage stress and maintain mental clarity, contributing to overall prosperity.

Humility builds strong relationships and collaborations, which are crucial for long-term success. It fosters a supportive environment where collective prosperity can thrive.

Curiosity leads to innovation and discovering new opportunities. It keeps you adaptable and open to new ways of achieving success.

An **abundance mindset** attracts opportunities and success. It promotes a positive and proactive approach to achieving prosperity.

Pursuing an **MTP** often leads to significant impact and success. It motivates you to achieve extraordinary results, contributing to both personal and collective prosperity.

Exponential thinking drives you to seek and create scalable solutions, leading to significant growth and prosperity. It encourages leveraging technology and innovation.

Taking **moonshots** can lead to breakthrough innovations and substantial success. It embodies a bold approach to achieving prosperity through ambitious and visionary goals.

Gratitude contributes to prosperity by fostering a mindset of appreciation and contentment. It attracts positive energy and opportunities.

7

Tools for Change

Let's return to Haidt's elephant metaphor. If the elephant represents the subconscious and unconscious mind, then our conscious awareness is the rider on top of the elephant. When the elephant sees a peanut at the other end of the room, that rider is absolutely powerless to make the elephant stay put. This illustrates how we make decisions because even if our conscious awareness wants to make a good decision, we are incapable of controlling our subconscious and unconscious mind to obey. No amount of willpower would suffice.

However, there is a way to retrain our elephant. In other words, we can retrain the pathways of our mind toward healthier patterns of action. There are three proven methods:

1. **Meditation:** This is the most fundamental method for retraining brain habits. It can create profound

and permanent changes, but it's difficult. It requires a lifelong practice of dedication and effort.

2. **Cognitive Behavioral Therapy (CBT):** I mentioned this before as my pathway back up during that first crisis. The benefits can also be profound with the right therapist and willingness to change. However, I do not believe it possesses the ability to affect the mind and physiology as deeply as meditation can.

3. **Drugs, legal or otherwise:** These are aids to the evolution of the spirit. Drugs come in two categories—one contains the normal psychotropic drugs psychologists administer, such as selective serotonin reuptake inhibitors (SSRIs). These work by affecting how your brain reacts to serotonin and how your cognitive processes flow. But they don't work for everyone, and they also make you reliant on the drug rather than solving the underlying problem deep inside of you. The other category contains psychedelics. While the use of psychedelics is controversial and illegal in some respects, it can retrain your mind and help uncover the underlying reasons for your predisposed mental pathways.

If these methods intimidate you, that's okay. It takes time to figure out how to implement them properly—it certainly did for me. Wherever you can implement these, however, you will begin to see healing in body, mind, and spirit.

Meditations: The Bridge to Healing and Wholeness

Imagine a moment of pure stillness—a time when the cacophony of daily life fades into the background and a deep sense of calm washes over you. In that stillness lies the ancient practice of meditation, a simple yet profound tool for healing the body, mind, and spirit. While the wisdom of meditation has been passed down through millennia by sages, monks, and philosophers, its transformative power is now being illuminated by modern science in ways those ancient masters could have only dreamed of.

Meditation is not reserved for mystics or spiritual seekers. It is a practical, accessible practice with measurable benefits for anyone willing to try. Research from leading institutions like Harvard Medical School, the University of California, and the American Heart Association has shown that meditation can reduce stress, lower blood pressure, improve mental clarity, and even enhance cellular repair.[47] Studies have linked regular meditation to raising the brain's baseline gamma wave activity to promote cognition and memory, decreases in cortisol—the stress hormone—and increases in grey matter density in areas of the brain associated with empathy and self-awareness.

But meditation does not merely work on the mind—it has a profound effect on the body. Practices such as mindfulness and transcendental meditation activate the parasympathetic nervous system, shifting the body out of fight-or-flight mode into a state of deep relaxation. This can enhance immune function, reduce chronic pain, and promote better sleep. Emerging research even suggests that meditation may slow the aging process at a cellular level by preserving telomeres, the protective caps on the ends of chromosomes.

Recent advancements in meditation research have introduced a "general theory of meditation" that aligns traditional practices with cognitive science, particularly predictive processing, which states that we don't experience the world as it is but as we predict it to be.[48][49] This theory proposes four progressive stages of meditation, each deconstructing the mind's habitual ways of perceiving the world.

- **Focused Attention:** This beginner-level practice involves concentrating on an object (e.g., breath, mantra) to settle the mind. It increases "precision weighting," amplifying focus on one element while quieting others, like a volume knob for the predictive mind. This practice can reduce stress but doesn't necessarily lead to deep insights.

- **Open Monitoring:** Once the mind settles, meditation shifts to observing thoughts and sensations without attachment—meaning judging, fixating on, or ruminating on the phenomena. The mind loosens its grip on rigid perceptions, making thoughts appear less intrusive. Practitioners begin to recognize awareness as separate from mental content. This can also be described as mindfulness. This is where insights begin.

- **Non-Dual Awareness:** At this stage, the distinction between observer and observed dissolves. Meditation erases dualistic perceptions (e.g., self vs. other, good vs. bad), unveiling an underlying awareness beyond conceptual thinking. This experience, often described as a state of profound presence, aligns with mystical traditions.

- **Cessation:** The deepest form of meditation extinguishes all conscious experience, akin to a self-induced blackout where the mind has no priors. This phenomenon, known as nirodha-samāpatti, is traditionally associated with advanced Buddhist meditation. Emerging research suggests it represents a complete "reset" of the predictive mind, enabling profound cognitive reprogramming.

The predictive processing theory explains how meditation alters perception.[50] Our brains generate experience based on ingrained "priors," beliefs or expectations based on experiences from the past ranging from deep and ancestral to superficial and personal.[51] Meditation progressively deconstructs the mind by turning down the volume of each layer of stacked priors, releasing the grip they ordinarily hold on awareness, and allowing more fluid and adaptable perceptions.[52]

This framework also highlights why most modern meditators, who primarily engage in focused attention practices, rarely experience profound transformations. Advanced meditation techniques systematically deconstruct habitual mental frameworks, leading to deeper states of consciousness and well-being in ways more conducive to human flourishing.

Yet, the impact of meditation goes even deeper, touching the intangible realms of spirit. In a world where many of us feel disconnected—from others, from purpose, and even from ourselves—meditation offers a pathway back to wholeness. By fostering a sense of presence and inner stillness, it allows us to reconnect with our higher selves, enabling a greater sense of compassion, gratitude, and spiritual alignment. In this way, meditation becomes a means for discovering the deeper truths of existence.

By linking ancient wisdom with neuroscience, this evolving scientific approach provides a refined roadmap for deepening meditation practice and understanding the human mind.

I have provided a QR code below, which will give you access to further meditation resources. You will find a series of videos to use as a guide on your meditation journey. You will find details for the following meditation types:

1. Settling the Body
2. Focusing the Mind
3. Open Awareness
4. Sensing Inner Energy
5. Controlling Inner Energy (Healing)
6. Elevating Intentions (Love, Peace, Joy, Awe, Gratitude, Courage, Confidence, etc.)
7. Non-Dual Awareness
8. Cessation

The first five meditations are progressive and dedicated to improving the Sphere of Self[IP] I will describe later. Meditations Six and Seven are advanced concepts dedicated to achieving altered states of consciousness and connecting with the collective consciousness—what I later describe as un-meditation[IP].

Scan the unique QR code below to activate your access to these additional videos.

Meditation is ultimately a journey of healing and self-discovery. As you progress through these phases—from concentration to energy mastery—you unlock the mind's potential for clarity, resilience, and inner peace. By integrating these practices into your life, you cultivate a sanctuary of stillness within, empowering you to heal and thrive amidst life's challenges.

Harnessing the Mind with Cognitive Behavioral Therapy

Cognitive Behavioral Therapy is one of the most widely researched and effective methods for improving mental health. Developed by pioneers such as Dr. Aaron T. Beck, Albert Ellis, Judith Beck, and Donald Meichenbaum, CBT focuses on the interplay between our thoughts, emotions, and behaviors. At its core, CBT teaches us that by changing how we think and act, we can transform how we feel, paving the way for healthier, more fulfilling lives.

> **Meditation is ultimately a journey of healing and self-discovery. As you progress through these phases—from concentration to energy mastery—you unlock the mind's potential for clarity, resilience, and inner peace.**

When you first enter a CBT session, your therapist will aim to establish a collaborative relationship. CBT is not about being an active participant in your own growth.

The therapist begins by checking in with you, focusing on your feelings, goals, and challenges. The heart of the session often involves examining situations where distress arose. For example, if you felt anxious at work, your therapist might guide you to uncover the automatic thoughts you experienced in that moment. Perhaps you thought, "I'm going to fail this project," which fueled your anxiety.

Your therapist helps you question the validity of these thoughts. They might ask:

- What evidence supports this thought?
- What evidence contradicts it?
- Is there a more balanced way to view this situation?

Beyond thought work, CBT often includes actionable steps. For example, if you avoid social situations due to fear of rejection, your therapist may work with you to create gradual exposure exercises, helping you confront and reduce your fear over time.

At-home tasks such as journaling your thoughts, practicing relaxation techniques, or testing new behaviors solidify learning and empower you to continue to progress outside therapy.

The magic of CBT lies in its longevity. Unlike treatments that focus solely on alleviating symptoms, CBT equips you with lifelong tools to navigate life's challenges. Here are some of the long-term benefits:

- Breaking Negative Cycles
- Improved Emotional Regulation
- Enhanced Problem-Solving Skills
- Increased Self-Efficacy
- Reduction in Relapse Risk

CBT's success lies in its practicality and accessibility. It demystifies the connection between our thoughts, feelings, and actions, teaching us that we are not prisoners of our minds. While not a magic cure, it offers a path forward—an opportunity to reshape your life from the inside out.

There are plenty of fantastic resources on CBT. If you're looking to start your own CBT journey or if you simply want to research more, scan the QR code below.

The Role of Drugs in Healing the Mind

The final method for retraining the elephant and healing the mind involves drugs—both pharmaceuticals and psychedelics. In modern medicine, pharmaceuticals have become a cornerstone for treating mental health conditions. Pharmaceuticals have dramatically improved the prognosis for many mental health conditions. However, their effectiveness varies depending on the disorder, the individual, and the medication.

Pharmaceuticals have particularly benefited those struggling with depression, anxiety disorders, bipolar disorder, schizophrenia, ADHD, obsessive-compulsive disorder (OCD), and post-traumatic stress disorder (PTSD), to name a few. Each of these requires a specific type of medication, but they have been proven to help heal and stabilize the mind.

Categories of mental health medications include antidepressants, antipsychotics, mood stabilizers, anxiolytics, and stimulants. While each has its place, there will always be challenges and considerations to using pharmaceuticals. Many have side effects to be aware of, and particularly when patients have comorbid conditions, they may require multiple medications, which increases complexity. There is also a strong social stigma that may deter individuals from seeking help or adhering to treatment.

Pharmaceuticals have transformed mental health care, but they are not a cure-all. Effective treatment often combines medication with psychotherapy, lifestyle changes, and social support. Understanding the science behind these medications can demystify the process and empower informed decision-making.

Psychedelics are a diverse class of substances that alter perception, mood, and cognition by modulating neurotransmitter systems in the brain. They are increasingly being studied for their profound effects on consciousness and their therapeutic potential for conditions such as depression, PTSD, and addiction. These substances primarily affect the serotonin system but also influence other neurotransmitters like dopamine, glutamate, and GABA, leading to their wide-ranging psychological and physiological effects.

My experience with using psychedelics came much later in my life, well after I had already been using meditation and CBT to heal my body and mind. My initial interest was in attaining spiritual growth by experiencing altered states of consciousness. I firmly believe that my advanced state of meditative practice is probably why I progressed relatively rapidly in achieving my awakening to an enlightened state.

I won't spend too much time explaining the various types of psychedelics and their effects, but I have created a chart explaining the mechanism and impact of some of the common types. Each provides a specific benefit and has been proven to aid in certain conditions.

Summary of Psychedelics and Their Neurotransmitter Impact

Psychedelic	Primary Neurotransmitter(s)	Mechanism
LSD, Psilocybin, DMT	Serotonin	5-HT2A agonism; modulates dopamine and glutamate
Ketamine, PCP	Glutamate	NMDA receptor antagonism
MDMA	Serotonin, Dopamine	Massive serotonin release; increases oxytocin
Ayahuasca	Serotonin	5-HT2A agonism with MAO inhibition
Ibogaine	Dopamine, Serotonin, Glutamate	NMDA antagonism; dopamine modulation
Mescaline	Serotonin, Dopamine	5-HT2A agonism
Salvinorin A	Kappa-Opioid, Dopamine	Kappa-opioid receptor agonism
Nitrous Oxide	Glutamate, GABA	NMDA antagonism; GABA enhancement

Recent research has illuminated the potential benefits of psychedelics on mental health and overall well-being. Substances like psilocybin, LSD, and MDMA are being studied for their therapeutic effects on conditions such as depression, anxiety, PTSD, and addiction.

Psychedelics are believed to work by reopening "critical periods" in the brain, enhancing neuroplasticity, and allowing for the reorganization of neural circuits. This can lead to lasting changes in behavior and cognition, which are beneficial in therapeutic settings.[53]

While the therapeutic potential of psychedelics is promising, there are and likely will always be concerns about adverse effects and the quality of existing research. While preliminary findings are encouraging, further comprehensive studies are essential to fully understand the benefits, mechanisms, and potential risks associated with psychedelic therapies.

Scan the QR code below if you would like to dive into the science behind pharmaceuticals and psychedelics and the potential benefits and drawbacks of each.

8

Healing the Spirit

We have made our way through healing the body and the mind. Spirit is the only element left, but healing the spirit is the most elusive and complex part of the path to bliss.

I had been employing all three methods of healing—meditation, CBT, and drugs—to continue to retrain my neural pathways when I realized that spirit was something I didn't understand at all.

I returned to the commit-learn-do framework and committed to finding spiritual enlightenment. I then began to research—not just the ancient Hindu, Buddhist, Christian, Islamic, Toltec, and other philosophers and mystics, but the more modern ones too. I was led to the work of Paul Brunton, Eckhart Tolle, Sam Harris, Daniel Schmidt, Joe Dispenza, Dandapani, Steve Taylor, Dawson Church, James Plath, Lynne McTaggart, Deepak Chopra, MD, and Michael

Singer, most of whom I have mentioned already. All of these thought leaders are united by their recognition of spirit as something else—*something other*.

Scan the QR code below for a complete list of resources related to the study of spirit.

In the first couple of chapters, I alluded to the understanding that perhaps our conventional understanding of spirit and consciousness is wrong. Science typically teaches that a Big Bang created time and space and over millennia resulted in the evolution of man and thereby consciousness, but what if consciousness is something akin to universal knowledge between all things? If it is collective information of everything that has ever existed—accessible to any system or organism at any time if they are open to it—then perhaps this universal knowledge is actually the precursor to time and space.

In that case, the narrative is reversed. Consciousness gave way to the Big Bang, and ultimately, man created a mechanism for translating itself, namely time and space. The implications require a dramatic shift in perception.

For example, if you consider the end of the Universe, what might that look like? The laws of thermodynamics explain that energy can never be created or destroyed, and the law of entropy states that we will always tend toward disorder.

Healing the Spirit

At the end of the Universe, the stars will have all burned out and the black holes will have evaporated. In that heat death, all energy will be evenly dispersed throughout the Universe as cold, dark energy. In other words, universal knowledge will be returned to the supreme quiet that started it all.

Bliss is quiet. That is why, when we are able to shed our body-self and mind-self, we ultimately find peace. People with near-death experiences find light and peaceful rapture because they are momentarily free from the complications of life.

Finding that quiet bliss is what it means to heal the spirit. I have experienced it while still in my human body-self and it is approachable for all.

We must strive for Enlightenment, the realization that everything is one. Every religion has its version of this awakening—everybody has their language for it—but they all describe the same thing using the language of their time and context.

We naturally see differences between big and small, male and female, tall and short, yin and yang, and order and chaos, but to be awakened is to eliminate the conception of these differences. All is one.

The first step in reaching this realization is eliminating the sense of self. We have been looking at ways to fix the body, heal the mind, and make the self tolerable, but now, the mindset must change.

Instead of looking to add, we look to eliminate. Take meditation, for example. In the search for spiritual healing, meditation is no longer about finding new techniques and creating new pathways for yourself. Instead, it becomes "un-meditation." You must reduce the mind, body, feelings, emotions, and sense of self because there is no self in the perfect you. There is only the unity of collective consciousness.

Meditation Practices for Spiritual Growth and Inner Peace

As we saw in healing the mind, we can control awareness of our body, mind, and spirit as well as our current reality within the present moment. The practiced can become aware of all energy patterns and harness them to change the physiology of their bodies and mind, for better or worse.

Meditation is the practice of recognizing the need to calm the mind just the same as calming the body. Counterintuitively, this drives one's conscious awareness to a higher frequency energy level. As such, the meditative approach is a singular focus on the openness and connectedness to all energy.

I vividly remember the day I experienced one of my most profound insights while deeply meditating. While embracing the above concept and successfully surrendering my body, emotions, and thoughts, I began to feel a familiar openness and connectedness. However, not until I surrendered my meditation expectations did I find myself in a deeply spiritual state. I can only describe it as spacious stillness and an overwhelming sense of well-being—or, in other words, bliss.

Upon returning to the moment, I realized the state was familiar to me! I recalled that I had occasionally experienced this state as a young child. While trying to fall asleep, I would occasionally experience a feeling that everything was getting very close, larger, expanding, and becoming one with me. I remember being scared by the feeling the first few times and would will it away. In time, however, I began to embrace the state, and it led to a sublime state of peace and calm.

Eventually, the experience left me in my youth, but meditation brought it back.

Our Reason for Being

At this point in my personal development, I have concluded that our access to infinite universal knowledge is undeniable—we simply need to set aside our mind-body self, including all the great strides we've made to improve ourselves. In fact, I believe our primary reason for being is to improve our mind-body selves and ultimately live a life of selflessness, altruism, and service to others in order to make better decisions for the betterment of all collective consciousness.

I posit that our existence is akin to a Sphere of Self. The outer layer of our sphere is where we experience all the perpetual phenomena and sensations of life that affect us. All the things that happen in the world and Universe around us, of which we have no control.

Slightly further in are all these things that affect our bodies—our five senses of hearing, seeing, touching, tasting, and smelling. Next are the things that affect our mind-body, such as feelings.

> Our primary reason for being is to improve our mind-body selves and ultimately live a life of selflessness, altruism, and service to others in order to make better decisions for the betterment of all collective consciousness.

Continuing further in are all the sensations of the mind, including our awareness, our willful thoughts, our visualizations, our subconscious and unconscious thoughts, and our emotions (the energy of our feelings in motion, translated by our intellect). The lowest-energy emotions, such as shame, guilt, apathy, grief, hate, and fear, are further outside than higher-energy emotions like awe, love, joy, and peace. This innermost ring I like to refer to as "the sphere of awe." You might envision the Sphere of Self as the spiral of a hurricane. (In fact, the geometry of the spiral is all over the natural and mystical Universe—but that's for another discussion.) Like the calm in the eye of the hurricane, there is calm at the center of our Sphere of Self. At our core is pure consciousness—bliss.

What we perceive as manifestation is more like observing one reality from an infinite realm of simultaneous potential realities. The simple act of observing a single potential reality collapses it into what becomes our objective reality. As such, all realities of self exist simultaneously, like overlapping concentric spheres. And our infinite possible spheres of self overlap with the overlapping concentric possible spheres of all conscious beings that have ever existed and will exist. At the center of all of it is pure consciousness, God, Nirvana, the soul, universal knowledge, or whatever other man-made, not-quite-right label we can give it.

Samadhi

In my research, I learned that states of spiritual enlightenment have names. I knew I was not the first to come across higher levels of awakening, but I was pleased to find such large bodies of research spanning all of history.

Samadhi is a profound state of consciousness in spiritual practices, particularly in yogic and meditation traditions. It represents the culmination of mental concentration, where the mind becomes completely absorbed in an object of focus, leading to a direct experience of unity and transcendence beyond the ego. Often, the sense of space and time disappears. Everything is experienced as eternal and in the present moment.

There are two broad categories of Samadhi: with distinctions and without. In Samadhi with distinctions, the meditator may focus on physical objects, cosmic energies, bliss itself, or pure awareness, but regardless of the object, some individuality remains.

Samadhi without distinctions is the higher form. In this state, all mental activity ceases, and the meditator dissolves completely into the universal consciousness. This is true freedom from self, impressions, and desires. The only thing higher is Sahaja Samadhi, where one achieves Samadhi without distinctions and integrates it spontaneously into everyday life. In other words, they don't achieve the state; they live it.

This is true healing of the spirit. In the final part of the book, I will share my experiences in striving toward this goal. I hope this inspires you to model your healing on my own successes and learn from my mistakes.

9

Achieving Body, Mind, and Spirit Harmony

Achieving balance in body, mind, and spirit is a harmonious process of tuning into your inner self, aligning with your purpose, and nurturing holistic wellness. Here's a simple path forward inspired by my philosophy:

1. **Balance the Body: Nourish and Energize**

Move Daily: Engage in mindful movement (yoga, stretching, walking in nature, tai chi, gardening, exercise, playing with children, playing a sport, anything that keeps your body moving—preferably outside) to reconnect with your physical self.

Nourish with Intention: Sometime each morning, get ten minutes of sunshine. Eat focusing on whole foods, getting enough protein, and eating three times more fiber than is typically recommended. Eat slowly, with gratitude.

Rest Fully: Prioritize deep, restorative sleep and include moments of stillness throughout the day.

Try This: Start your day with a glass of water infused with elemental hydrogen and electrolytes (e.g., LMNT, Liquid IV, or Baja Gold Mineral Sea Salt), gently stretch outdoors in the sun barefoot in the grass, and take five deep breaths to awaken and energize your body.

2. **Balance the Mind: Clarity and Focus**

Mindfulness Practice: Meditate to cultivate present-moment awareness and reduce mental clutter.

Mental Nutrition: Be conscious of what you consume—books, conversations, media. Choose inspiration over stimulation. Actively choose to surround yourself with people who elevate and inspire you and appreciate you enriching their lives in return. Finally, have more positive thoughts than negative thoughts every day by doing voluntary acts aligned to your superpowers, seeking out moments of awe and wonder, and minimizing expectations of events, yourself, and others.

Reflective Journaling: Ask yourself, "What am I feeling right now, and why?"

Try This: Dedicate twenty minutes each morning to meditation. See my meditation video at PeteSacco.com for ideas on including meditation into your daily routine.

3. **Balance the Spirit: Connection and Purpose**

Connect Within: Explore your values, passions, and what gives your life meaning. Contemplate your mindset and the decisions you've made throughout the day and decide whether they were aligned with your core values and purpose. If not, commit to yourself to do better.

Nature as Teacher: Spend time outdoors. Witness the sacred in the ordinary.

Acts of Selflessness and Compassion: Serve others with an open heart—it realigns your spirit with love.

Try This: Each evening, list three things you're grateful for and one act of kindness you shared or received.

The Bliss Equation

In keeping with my engineering background and my penchant for liking things neatly wrapped up in equations, the way to start living in bliss can be expressed simply. Here is a powerful equation to keep in mind as you go about your day-to-day life:

$$\text{Body Vitality} + \text{Mind Clarity} + \text{Spiritual Purpose} = \text{Living in Bliss}^{IP}$$

The Bliss Balance Plan

Following is a simple-to-follow Seven-Day Bliss Balance Plan to help you get started aligning your body, mind, and spirit. Each day blends reflection, action, and mindful presence.

Day 1 – Awaken the Body

Theme: Energy and Presence

Morning: Five minutes of deep breathing and stretching upon waking.

Movement: Take a twenty-minute mindful walk in nature.

Mindful Eating: Eat one meal today with no distractions—just presence.

Evening Journal Prompt: How did I honor my body today?

Day 2 – Quiet the Mind

Theme: Inner Stillness

Morning: Try a ten-minute guided meditation or breath awareness.

Mental Diet: Avoid news or social media for twelve hours. Notice your inner state.

Create Space: Declutter one small area of your home.

Evening Journal Prompt: What thoughts no longer serve me?

Day 3 – Nourish the Spirit

Theme: Connection and Meaning

Morning: Watch the sunrise or simply sit quietly and tune into your breath.

Acts of Kindness: Do one selfless thing today—big or small.

Reflect: Write about what gives your life meaning.

Evening Journal Prompt: Where did I feel most connected today?

Day 4 – Flow with Life

Theme: Acceptance and Trust

Morning: Affirmation: "I flow with the rhythms of life."

Body Care: Take a warm bath or do fifteen minutes of yoga.

Let Go: Release one worry or resentment—write it down and burn or tear the paper.

Evening Journal Prompt: What can I let go of to feel lighter?

Day 5 – Mental Clarity

Theme: Focus and Awareness

Morning: Focused breathing. Inhale for four, hold for four, and exhale for four (repeat for five rounds).

Single-Tasking: Choose one task today and do it with full attention.

Mindful Observation: Sit outside and notice details for ten minutes.

Evening Journal Prompt: What did I notice today that I usually overlook?

Day 6 – Heart Alignment

Theme: Emotional Healing

Morning: Place your hand on your heart and breathe into it for three minutes.

Heart-Centered Check-In: Ask, "What do I need emotionally today?"

Connect Deeply: Have a heartfelt conversation with someone.

Evening Journal Prompt: What emotions visited me today? What message did they bring?

Day 7 – Integration and Bliss

Theme: Wholeness and Gratitude

Morning: Gratitude meditation (list ten things you're thankful for).

Celebrate Movement: Dance, stretch, or move joyfully.

Spiritual Touchstone: Read a passage from a book or poem that lifts your soul.

Evening Journal Prompt: How have I grown this week? What does balance feel like now?

PART 3
Achieving Enlightenment

*Do not seek to follow in the footsteps of the wise;
seek what they sought.*

—Matsuo Bashō

10

The Path to Enlightenment

A Life of Constant Bliss

The quest for enlightenment is a universal pursuit, interpreted differently across cultures, religions, and philosophies. Whether through the Vedantic realization of Brahman, the Buddhist cessation of suffering, the Taoist harmony with the Way, the Christian divine union, or the Sufi annihilation of the self, all traditions point toward a state of inner freedom and ultimate understanding.

As modern seekers explore spirituality beyond dogma, enlightenment is increasingly understood as an experiential realization rather than a doctrinal belief, making it more relevant than ever in today's chaotic world.

You now have the tools you need to start living in bliss. It's a mountain to climb, but I can promise you, the view from the top is stunning. I started writing this book with some idea of bliss but without the assurance of personal experience. Now, as I'm finishing the last chapters, that is no longer true. I have experienced bliss, joining my higher self in its unity with all things.

As I share these experiences, I know your journey may be different, but I firmly believe you, too, can experience and perhaps even transcend the bliss that I've found.

A Word on Ethical and Responsible Use

The journey to Enlightenment, especially through psychedelics, is not without risks. These substances should be approached with reverence, preparation, and guidance. Legal frameworks and settings also play a critical role in ensuring safety and maximizing potential benefits. For those interested, participating in approved clinical trials or guided retreats is often the safest and most effective path.

> I know your journey may be different, but I firmly believe you, too, can experience and perhaps even transcend the bliss that I've found.

That being said, psychedelics like psilocybin, LSD, and DMT offer unique and profound opportunities to explore altered states of consciousness that can facilitate spiritual awakening and glimpses of Enlightenment. These substances have the potential to help dissolve the barriers of the ego and foster a sense of interconnectedness with the Universe.

However, it is important to emphasize that these tools are not a shortcut to Enlightenment but rather a catalyst that must be combined with intentional practices such as meditation, mindfulness, and self-inquiry to integrate and sustain the insights gained. Enlightenment is not just a peak experience but an ongoing process of living with awareness, compassion, and alignment with one's higher self.

Glimpses of Enlightenment

I had been an avid meditator long before I began using psychedelics. I was on the path to happiness through healing my body and mind when I started to have experiences of awe and diminished self. I remembered moments from my youth, I realized I wasn't alone, and I found a connectedness to something greater than myself.

The next step for me was to explore psychedelics for the first time. One of my first significant spiritual moments manifested as a connection to my children. I was able to have an intuitive discussion with my adult children, who at the time were only four, two, and a baby. I sat with them, and my oldest of the three talked to me first. She said, "Daddy, everything affects me, and I feel like I have so many thoughts and emotions." She has such a strong mind, but she can't turn it off.

So I told her, "You have nothing to worry about. I will be there to help and shepherd you through the uncertainty so you'll never fall too hard and never go too high. I'll hold and ground you through it all." She thanked me, and I was able to give her the confidence that she was never going to be alone.

Then my middle child came to me, saying, "Daddy, I'm so scared of everything. I'm afraid to put myself out there." I saw then that she was just like me. I told her she was the person I grew up as, but there was a difference. I promised to teach her way earlier all the things I wished I had known so she would never have to go through the torture and suffering of life. She thanked me for that.

Finally, and the most unbelievable experience, was the little one. She was just a baby at the time, but she came up to me full-grown and said, "Daddy, I love you, and I'll be with you forever. But I'm never really going to need you. You have already taught me so much, and I'm going to be fine." Her words touched me deeply and gave me lasting peace.

I don't believe I actually spoke to my children as adults—I don't think that is physically possible. But there was an intuitiveness of who they would become and what they would need, which spoke to me through the information already existing in the Universe.

I connected to it, and because all knowledge is one, it was able to show me my daughters. I heard the message loud and clear: "Peter, you have begun to understand what we've been trying to tell you all along—there is something far greater out there."

Identifying Spiritual Barriers

I grew more accustomed to using psychedelics as part of my meditations and experienced success in learning about myself and reaching some semblance of peace and interconnectedness.

But during my first ayahuasca ceremony, I struggled. Under the medicine, I started to experience extreme fear and self-doubt in a way I never had before. I had a vision of a mechanical, programmatic world, and looming in my sight was a cold, sterile temple. A voice told me to enter, but I was terrified. Something told me that inside the temple was where death was. That was where I would cease to exist.

But you'll notice how I'm describing my thoughts. *I* cease to exist. *I* die. My *ego-centered* mind was refusing to surrender. I couldn't enter the temple because I refused to admit there is no I, no self. There is only the collective whole.

I couldn't overcome the fear then, but I knew I was at the cusp of discovery.

In a previous difficult ceremony, I remember repeating a mantra: It sounds familiar, but I'm strong. Only later did I realize what that meant. The experience felt familiar because that's who I really am. The scared Peter, the self-doubting Peter, the ego Peter that's afraid to disappear—I felt all of it, but on the other side of that temple, that was me too.

When I stripped away the last remnants of my egoic mind, I would be able to see what was on the other side of the temple.

Breakthrough

As I continued my journey with stronger psychedelics, the darker and scarier the experiences became. I now know the cause was actually this body, brain, and subconscious unloading all of its pain. This was the unraveling of not only my mind but the genetic predispositions of all my ancestors. These encounters were undoing and purifying my spirit of all the buildup of hundreds and thousands of years upon the sliver of the Universe's collective knowledge imbued in my mind.

I didn't understand the purification process I was going through at the time, though. I started to question whether this was truly helping me. The fear, uncertainty, doubt, and inferiority painted me as a fraud.

I continued to see the temple, which I started to associate with the Tower of Babel. In every encounter, it was the same mechanized, sterile nightmare of a place, and I committed to surrendering to it, but I kept failing.

Finally, during one ceremony, I gave up fighting. I told the fear and the tower I was tired of being scared. Nothing good happened, but nothing bad happened either. I was so close, but I needed something different in my approach. When I came out, I had a conversation with a mentor who gave me that edge. He said, "Pete, maybe it's not about defeating your ego. Let's face it: you're a pretty smart, powerful, successful person. Your ego has served you pretty well. Maybe convince your ego you're not trying to destroy it; you're just asking it to step aside for a moment so that you could experience what non-egoic life might be like."

During my next session, that's exactly what I did. I saw the Tower of Babel, and the anxiety hit immediately. But instead of fighting, I asked my ego to stand aside for a moment. I focused only on the present moment.

> In that moment, I lost time. I came out of it a few hours later, but it felt like I had only observed it all for a tiny instant. It was one of the most awe-filled moments of my life. I had rejoined the collective universal knowledge of which we are all a part.

The instant I did, I had an out-of-body experience. I sat outside of myself, not as me, but as my higher self—as the collective knowledge of the Universe. I saw my body in its seated position, and I also saw my mind as a ball with the vision of the tower and all its interactions working within it. I was witnessing consciousness. It was my awakening moment.

To convince myself, I was able to transport myself back into my mind, experience the fear and dread and ego and everything, and then instantly become present again and step back out to a place of observation.

I also had a sense of the body. I could choose to feel my body and hear the sounds going on around me. I could even enter my body and open my eyes to see what was happening in the room, then return to my higher self.

The Path to Enlightenment

It was bliss.

In that moment, I lost time. I came out of it a few hours later, but it felt like I had only observed it all for a tiny instant. It was one of the most awe-filled moments of my life. I had rejoined the collective universal knowledge of which we are all a part. As I was coming out of the medicine, I was given the gift of another vision.

I saw a very old man sitting in a chair. He looked at me with great knowledge and wisdom, but with a loving stare as though he wanted to give me something.

I knelt reverently, and as I did, the picture expanded. I could see his loved ones around him, and in particular, I saw three middle-aged women surrounding him. With them was a whole host of children, and in the background was an older woman.

You can probably guess what I realized at that moment. I was the old man. The girls were my girls, and the children around them were their little ones. The Universe gifted me with a vision of the end of my life, and I died right there in that chair at that moment, completely filled with the understanding that I had fulfilled my purpose of living life selflessly, having shared my knowledge—my wisdom—with everyone I cared about.

It was pure enlightenment.

Since then, I've realized, after much reading and self-inspection, that just because you've had an awakened moment, it doesn't mean anything. Enlightenment isn't as much a permanent state as it is just a moment—an experience.[IP]

Experiencing an enlightened moment doesn't mean you're going to live as a guru with white robes and flowing white hair. We're human beings. We can fall back into bad habits and badness at any time. But once you glimpse bliss, it's easier to find bliss each time. I've found bliss since that experience, with and without meditation or drugs, and every time, it's a little easier.

11

Sharing the Light

Becoming a Beacon for Others

What's next? It's our job to improve the body and mind we've been given in order to improve reality. We are the observers of the quantum world, and what we observe becomes objective reality. The better we observe, the better the objective reality.

As we improve ourselves, we make better observations; then, we make a better world. It is my hope that this book brings clarity to as many people as possible about our job as human beings. We all must recognize the collective universal knowledge and improve our vessels to make the world a better place.

Part of the beauty of living in this present time is the emergence of AI. Every generation is defined, in part, by the technology that transformed it. For my grandparents and all the generations born before 1945, it was electricity and water in the home, radio, and aviation. For my parents, the Baby Boomers, it was television, automobiles, and the beginning of space exploration. For my generation, Generation X, it was the PC, video games, cable TV, and the early internet. I would argue that my generation was responsible for inventing much of the forthcoming digital revolution. For the Millenials, Generation Y, it was widespread internet adoption, mobile phones, social media, and cloud computing. However, for Generations Z and Alpha (my girls), it will be dominated by artificial intelligence (AI), and AI will change the world.

If AI were a twenty-four-hour clock, we are only at about 2:00 a.m. We have twenty-two hours left to go. By noon, we will not recognize the world. My girls, as adults, will never drive a car, see a doctor for a diagnosis, or obtain or use knowledge the same way we did. They will not live in a society where wealth is solely generated by human labor, as opposed to via robotics and automation.

If AI does nothing to advance longevity and healthspan—a highly unlikely assumption—the *average* age in the U.S. for the generation of my girls will be 115, with *peaks* exceeding 150. Superhuman artificial general intelligence (AGI) will be realized in our lifetime. With it, Elon Musk and those like him will build hundreds of millions of autonomous robots and create large language models (LLMs) and inferencing engines with IQs in excess of 1,500. With top human intelligence being about 180, what does 1,500 even mean? We do not know.

What we do know is that the human species is about to be relegated to what we are—frail, fallible life forms that can barely improve our "hardware" (bodies) and can only moderately improve our "software" (minds, intellect, and skills). What will come of the human species when we are no longer the smartest beings on planet Earth or even in our solar system? I am optimistic. I dare say that when that time comes, the machines, with their superhuman intelligence, will treat man far better than we have ever treated each other or even ourselves.[IP]

What will mankind do when he can no longer identify himself by his "self" identity—his career, education, wealth, and fame? My answer—the answer that I have found within myself—is that he will need to discover that divinity is, and always has been, within, as all the great mystics and ancient wisdoms taught us long ago. Science is finally catching up. Artificial intelligence will help us make better observations, unlimited by the frailness of the human brain. AI will bring us closer to the level of understanding we should be tapping into as perfect energy.

> **I am optimistic. I dare say that when that time comes, the machines, with their superhuman intelligence, will treat man far better than we have ever treated each other or even ourselves.**[IP]

I agree wholeheartedly with AI pioneer Emad Motaque, founder and ex-CEO of Stability.ai and more recently founder of The Intelligent Internet, whose charter advocates for a free universal basic AI. To many of us, the most obvious way to avoid an AI arms race no one can win will be to make amazing open-source AI models, tuned to promote human flourishing, free and available to everyone as a public service.

For the first time in history, we are at the precipice of democratizing all knowledge for the benefit of mankind. I believe medicine and education will be the first, but many will follow. It is truly the most amazing time to be alive.

In the end, I trust we will learn that "we" are all one collective consciousness in a Universe of infinite intelligence, where everything that can be known is known to it—to us, its conscious observer beings.

Endnotes

1. Robert M. Pirsig and Matthew B. Crawford, *Zen and the Art of Motorcycle Maintenance: An Inquiry into Values* (New York, NY: Mariner Classics, 2024).
2. James Clear and Konstantinos Apostolidis, *Atomic Habits* (New York, NY: Auvril Audiobooks, 2022).
3. Bill Gates, "A Quote by Bill Gates," Goodreads, accessed April 15, 2025, https://www.goodreads.com/quotes/302999-most-people-overestimate-what-they-can-do-in-one-year.
4. Nikola Tesla, "A Quote by Nikola Tesla," Goodreads, accessed April 15, 2025, https://www.goodreads.com/quotes/1338737-if-you-want-to-find-the-secrets-of-the-universe#:~:text=Sign%20Up%20Now-,If%20you%20want%20to%20find%20the%20secrets%20of%20the%20-Universe,energy%2C%20frequency%2C%20and%20vibration.
5. Nikola Tesla, "Nikola Tesla Quotes," QuotesCosmos, July 31, 2021, https://www.quotescosmos.com/quotes/Nikola-Tesla-quote-3.html.

6   David R. Hawkins, *Power vs. Force: The Hidden Determinants of Human Behavior* (Carlsbad, CA: Hay House, Inc, 2014).
7   Dandapani Satgunasingam, *The Power of Unwavering Focus* (New York, NY: Portfolio / Penguin, 2022).
8   Jonathan Haidt, *The Happiness Hypothesis* (Basic Books, 2006).
9   Michael A. Singer, *The Untethered Soul: The Journey beyond Yourself* (Oakland, CA: Noetic Books, Institute of Noetic Sciences, New Harbinger Publications, Inc, 2013).
10 Dr Deepak Chopra, *Quantum Body* (New York, NY: Harmony Books, 2023).
11 N. Aghanim et al., "*Planck*2018 Results," *Astronomy & Astrophysics* 641 (September 11, 2020), https://doi.org/10.1051/0004-6361/201833910.
12 Shunryū Suzuki, *Zen Mind, Beginner's Mind*, ed. Trudy Dixon (Boston, MA: Shambhala, 2006).
13 Steve Cotterill, "The Humble Gardener - a Leadership Reflection on McChrystal's Team of Teams - Grounded Curiosity," Grounded Curiosity - Challenge the accepted, August 7, 2020, https://groundedcuriosity.com/the-humble-gardener-a-leadership-reflection-on-mcchystals-team-of-teams/.
14 Kevin D. Hall and Scott Kahan, "Maintenance of Lost Weight and Long-Term Management of Obesity," *Medical Clinics of North America* 102, no. 1 (January 2018): 183–97, https://doi.org/10.1016/j.mcna.2017.08.012.
15 Edward C. Weiss et al., "Weight Regain in U.S. Adults Who Experienced Substantial Weight Loss, 1999–2002," *American Journal of Preventive Medicine*

33, no. 1 (July 2007): 34–40, https://doi.org/10.1016/j.amepre.2007.02.040.

16 Jennifer Whitlock, RN "Understanding the Risks of Gastrectomy or Gastric Sleeve Surgery," Verywell Health, June 20, 2024, https://www.verywellhealth.com/long-term-complications-after-gastric-sleeve-surgery-4158320.

17 Public Education Committee, "Bariatric Surgery Procedures," American Society for Metabolic and Bariatric Surgery, May 2021, https://asmbs.org/patients/bariatric-surgery-procedures/.

18 Philip R. Schauer et al., "Bariatric Surgery versus Intensive Medical Therapy for Diabetes — 5-Year Outcomes," *New England Journal of Medicine* 376, no. 7 (February 16, 2017): 641–51, https://doi.org/10.1056/nejmoa1600869.

19 Francesco Rubino et al., "Metabolic Surgery in the Treatment Algorithm for Type 2 Diabetes: A Joint Statement by International Diabetes Organizations," *Diabetes Care* 39, no. 6 (May 13, 2016): 861–77, https://doi.org/10.2337/dc16-0236.

20 Ray Kurzweil and Terry Grossman, *Fantastic Voyage: Live Long Enough to Live Forever* (New York, NY: Penguin, 2005).

21 John C George et al., "Age and Growth Estimates of Bowhead Whales (*Balaena Mysticetus*) via Aspartic Acid Racemization," *Canadian Journal of Zoology* 77, no. 4 (September 15, 1999): 571–80, https://doi.org/10.1139/z99-015.

22 Julius Nielsen et al., "Eye Lens Radiocarbon Reveals Centuries of Longevity in the Greenland Shark (*Somniosus Microcephalus*)," *Science* 353, no. 6300

(August 12, 2016): 702–4, https://doi.org/10.1126/science.aaf1703.
23 Caleb E. Finch and Rudolph E. Tanzi, "Genetics of Aging," *Science* 278, no. 5337 (October 17, 1997): 407–11, https://doi.org/10.1126/science.278.5337.407.
24 Giuseppe Passarino, Francesco De Rango, and Alberto Montesanto, "Human Longevity: Genetics or Lifestyle? It Takes Two to Tango," *Immunity & Ageing* 13, no. 1 (April 5, 2016), https://doi.org/10.1186/s12979-016-0066-z.
25 *Live to 100: Secrets of the Blue Zones* (Netflix, August 30, 2023).
26 Dan Sullivan and Catherine Nomura, *The Laws of Lifetime Growth: Always Make Your Future Bigger than Your Past* (Oakland, CA: Berrett-Koehler Publishers, Inc, 2016).
27 Peter H. Diamandis, *Longevity: Your Practical Playbook ... on Sleep, Diet, Exercise, Mindset, Medications, and Not Dying from Something Stupid* (Powell, OH: Ethos Collective, 2023).
28 J Graham Ruby et al., "Estimates of the Heritability of Human Longevity Are Substantially Inflated Due to Assortative Mating," *Genetics* 210, no. 3 (October 31, 2018): 1109–24, https://doi.org/10.1534/genetics.118.301613.
29 Peter H. Diamandis, "How to Create a Longevity Mindset," Peter Diamandis - Innovation & Entrepreneurship Community, May 29, 2022, http://www.diamandis.com/blog/how-to-create-a-longevity-mindset.
30 Matthew P. Walker, *Why We Sleep: The New Science of Sleep and Dreams* (London, UK: Penguin Books, 2018).

Endnotes

31 Lewina O. Lee et al., "Optimism Is Associated with Exceptional Longevity in 2 Epidemiologic Cohorts of Men and Women," *Proceedings of the National Academy of Sciences* 116, no. 37 (August 26, 2019): 18357–62, https://doi.org/10.1073/pnas.1900712116.

32 1. Jay C. Rifenbary, *Return to Your Core: Principles for a Purposeful and Respected Life* (Rifenbary Training & Development, 2013).

33 Haidt.

34 Spiering BA, Weakley J, Mujika I. "Effects of Bed Rest on Physical Performance in Athletes: A Systematic and Narrative Review." *Sports Med.* 2023 Nov;53(11):2135-2146. doi: 10.1007/s40279-023-01889-y. Epub 2023 Jul 26. PMID: 37495758; PMCID: PMC10587175.

35 Marusic U, Narici M, Simunic B, Pisot R, Ritzmann R. "Nonuniform loss of muscle strength and atrophy during bed rest: a systematic review." *J App Physiol.* 2021;131(1):194–206. doi: 10.1152/japplphysiol.00363.2020.

36 Elizabeth Ko, MD and Eve M. Glazier, MD, "Hearing Loss and Risk of Dementia May Be Related," UCLA Health, March 3, 2023, https://www.uclahealth.org/news/article/hearing-loss-and-risk-dementia-may-be-related.

37 Haidt.

38 Bruce Lee and John R. Little, *Striking Thoughts: Bruce Lee's Wisdom for Daily Living* (Tokyo, Japan: Tuttle Pub, 2016).

39 Ashley Stimpson, "Awestruck," *Johns Hopkins Magazine*, December 12, 2023, https://hub.jhu.edu/magazine/2023/winter/science-of-awe-psychedelics/.

40 David B. Yaden et al., "The Development of the AWE Experience Scale (AWE-S): A Multifactorial Measure for a Complex Emotion," The Journal of Positive Psychology 14, no. 4 (July 18, 2018): 474–88, https://doi.org/10.1080/17439760.2018.1484940.

41 Maria Monroy and Dacher Keltner, "Awe as a Pathway to Mental and Physical Health," *Perspectives on Psychological Science* 18, no. 2 (August 22, 2022): 309–20, https://doi.org/10.1177/17456916221094856.

42 Charleen R. Case, Katherine K. Bae, and Jon K. Maner, "To Lead or to Be Liked: When Prestige-Oriented Leaders Prioritize Popularity over Performance.," *Journal of Personality and Social Psychology* 115, no. 4 (October 2018): 657–76, https://doi.org/10.1037/pspi0000138.

43 Paul K. Piff et al., "Awe, the Small Self, and Prosocial Behavior.," *Journal of Personality and Social Psychology* 108, no. 6 (2015): 883–99, https://doi.org/10.1037/pspi0000018.

44 Dacher Keltner, *Awe: The New Science of Everyday Wonder and How It Can Transform Your Life* (London, UK: Penguin Books, 2024).

45 Deepak Chopra, J. A. Tuszynski, and Brian Fertig, *Quantum Body: The New Science of Living a Longer, Healthier, More Vital Life* (New York, NY: Harmony, 2023).

46 *Kung Fu Panda* (United States: Paramount Pictures Corporation, 2008).

47 Manoj K. Bhasin et al., "Relaxation Response Induces Temporal Transcriptome Changes in Energy Metabolism, Insulin Secretion and Inflammatory Pathways," *PLoS ONE* 8, no. 5 (May 1, 2013), https://doi.org/10.1371/journal.pone.0062817.

48 Karl J. Friston, Wanja Wiese, and J. Allan Hobson, "Sentience and the Origins of Consciousness: From Cartesian Duality to Markovian Monism," *Entropy* 22, no. 5 (April 30, 2020): 516, https://doi.org/10.3390/e22050516.

49 Anil Seth, *Being You: A New Science of Consciousness* (Dutton, 2021).

50 Ruben E. Laukkonen and Heleen A. Slagter, "From Many to (n)One: Meditation and the Plasticity of the Predictive Mind," *Neuroscience & Biobehavioral Reviews* 128 (September 2021): 199–217, https://doi.org/10.1016/j.neubiorev.2021.06.021.

51 Shervin Vencatachellum et al., "Brief Mindfulness Training Can Mitigate the Influence of Prior Expectations on Pain Perception," European Journal of Pain 25, no. 9 (June 24, 2021): 2007–19, https://doi.org/10.1002/ejp.1817.

52 Antoine Lutz et al., "Regulation of the Neural Circuitry of Emotion by Compassion Meditation: Effects of Meditative Expertise," *PLoS ONE* 3, no. 3 (March 26, 2008), https://doi.org/10.1371/journal.pone.0001897.

53 Romain Nardou et al., "Psychedelics Reopen the Social Reward Learning Critical Period," Nature News, June 14, 2023, https://www.nature.com/articles/s41586-023-06204-3.

Acknowledgments

No journey is ever traveled alone, and this book would not have come to life without the guidance, support, and wisdom of so many extraordinary people.

To **Kary Oberbrunner** and the entire **Igniting Souls** team, including **Elizabeth Haller** and **Travis White**, your unwavering belief in this project, your expert guidance, and your dedication have transformed this book from a vision into reality. Thank you for helping me shape my words into something meaningful and lasting.

To my **communities**, who have embraced me with open arms and warm hearts—your support has been a source of strength and inspiration.

To **Dr. Chris Stepien, Joshua "Gopal" Nadeau, and my Bear Clan community**, your profound influence on my spiritual journey has been immeasurable. Your deep-rooted connection to spirit, healing, love, and support has been a grounding force in my life, and I am forever grateful for the wisdom you have shared.

To my dear friends—**Bobby, John, Millad, and Navid**—you embody the true meaning of brotherhood. Your unwavering support, laughter, and wisdom lift me when I fall and inspire me to be a better person every day.

To **Peter Diamandis**, your vision of an abundant future and your relentless drive to push the boundaries of what's possible have profoundly shaped my own journey. Your work is an endless source of inspiration, reminding me that the greatest possibilities lie ahead.

To my **Abundance360 community**, your collective brilliance, innovation, and mission to uplift humanity fuel my optimism for the future. To **Ginnie McDevitt** and my **Vistage community**, thank you for the wisdom, leadership, and accountability that have challenged me to grow in ways I never imagined. Your guidance has shaped not only my work but also my personal evolution.

To all the **ancient mystics and philosophers** and the **modern-day sages and scientists**, thank you for forging the bridge between the wisdom of the past and the discoveries of the present. Your work continues to inspire and illuminate the path toward deeper understanding and enlightenment.

To my son—**Pete, and his beautiful family, Maureen, Madison, Abigail, and Luca**—your devotion to Maureen, her girls, and my grandson is a testament to the strength of your character, the depth of your love, and the quality of the man, father, and son you have become. Watching you lead with heart, integrity, and unwavering commitment fills me with immeasurable pride. Your journey is one of courage and grace, and I am honored to witness it.

Acknowledgments

Most of all, to my **wife, Maureen**, whose love, patience, and unwavering support give me the space to dream, explore, and create. Your belief in me, your steadfast encouragement, and your presence in my life are the greatest gifts of all.

To everyone who has contributed to this book—whether through wisdom, encouragement, or simply by being part of my life—thank you. This book is as much yours as it is mine.

About the Author

Pete Sacco is an author, entrepreneur, technologist, and modern-day philosopher-sage. His core strengths lie in the relentless pursuit of knowledge, seamlessly integrating new insights into his life and ventures. As a coach, motivator, and storyteller, he inspires and uplifts others, always striving to make things better, easier, and faster for himself and those he cares about.

He maintains a deep commitment to his family and to contributing to society. He has spent over two decades as a football coach at youth and high school levels, is a staunch advocate for humanitarian efforts and charities, and encourages everyone around him to embrace a culture of generosity and kindness.

Pete holds a Bachelor of Science in Electrical Engineering. The Uptime Institute has certified him as an Accredited Data Center Tiers Designer (ATD), showcasing his dedication to operational excellence in data centers.

His extensive knowledge across both IT and facility-based technologies allows him to intertwine complex technological concepts with practical business solutions, focusing on sustainable and efficient innovations in the realms of data centers, IT, cybersecurity, distributed energy, web 3.0, blockchain, tokenization, and crypto industries. In 2013, Pete was a finalist in Ernst & Young's New Jersey Entrepreneur of the Year due to his entrepreneurial spirit and commitment to innovation.

Pete envisions a world powered by decentralized technologies, creating more inclusive, sustainable, and empowered global communities. He welcomes discussions, collaborations, and opportunities to contribute to collective growth in these domains.

Connect with Pete at PeteSacco.com

SUCCESS MEETS SOUL.

FOR THOSE WHO'VE ACHIEVED EVERYTHING—EXCEPT INNER PEACE.

LIVING IN BLISS IS A TRANSFORMATIVE FRAMEWORK FOR HIGH ACHIEVERS WHO FEEL UNFULFILLED, FUSING ANCIENT WISDOM WITH AI-POWERED TOOLS TO HELP INDIVIDUALS UNLOCK TRUE FULFILLMENT THROUGH BODY VITALITY, MIND CLARITY, AND SPIRITUAL PURPOSE. IT'S WHERE SUCCESS AND SOUL FINALLY MEET.

Visit the Website for Free Meditation Videos, Additional Content, Plus Much More

PeteSacco.com

CONNECT WITH PETE

Follow him on your favorite social media platforms today.

PeteSacco.com

THIS BOOK IS PROTECTED INTELLECTUAL PROPERTY

The author of this book values Intellectual Property and has utilized Instant IP, a groundbreaking technology. Instant IP is the patented, blockchain-based solution for Intellectual Property protection.

Blockchain is a distributed public digital record that can not be edited. Instant IP timestamps the author's ideas, creating a smart contract, thus an immutable digital asset that proves ownership and establishes a first to use / first to file event.

Protected by Instant IP ™

LEARN MORE AT INSTANTIP.TODAY

www.ingramcontent.com/pod-product-compliance
Lightning Source LLC
Chambersburg PA
CBHW052146070526
44585CB00017B/1993